SOLDIER'S HEART

Art by Richard G. Lawrence, Combat Vietnam Veteran, U.S.M.C.

SOLDIER'S HEART

Survivors' Views of Combat Trauma

Edited by Sarah Hansel, Ph.D.,
Ann Steidle, R.N., Grace Zaczek, M.P.H.,
and Ron Zaczek, Veteran, U.S.M.C.

THE SIDRAN PRESS
LUTHERVILLE, MD

The views expressed by individual contributors to this book do not necessarily represent the policies and opinions of the National Trauma Institute at Baltimore, Inc., The Sidran Press, or The Sidran Foundation for Mental Illness. Contributor's comments about therapy should not be considered medical advice. The editors and publisher of this volume recommend that readers follow the advice of a physician who is directly involved in their care or the care of a member of their family.

Grateful acknowledgment is made for permission to reprint "Loss of Innocence" and "Vet Center," and to print excerpts from the poetry and essays of Thomas N. Bills, Copyright © 1993 by Thomas N. Bills, and reprinted by permission of the author.

Grateful acknowledgment is made for permission to print excerpts from "On Clarendon," "Disability Morning," and "Experience of Transference," Copyright © 1988 by Edward J. Burris, and reprinted by permission of the author.

Grateful acknowledgment is made for permission to print the work of Daniel D., Copyright © 1988 by Daniel D., and reprinted by permission of the author.

Grateful acknowledgment is made for permission to print excerpts from "Letters From Home," Copyright © 1993 by Michael Harac, and reprinted by permission of the author.

Grateful acknowledgment is made to George Hill and to *The Gainesville Sun* for permission to print "Sharing the Struggles of a Friend" and "Hill 55," Copyright © 1992 and 1993 by George Hill, and reprinted by permission of the author.

Grateful acknowledgment is made for permission to print excerpts from "Where Light Is As Darkness," Copyright © 1991 by Kellan Kyllo, and reprinted by permission of the author.

Grateful acknowledgment is made for permission to publish the art of Sgt. Richard G. Lawrence, Combat Vietnam Veteran, U.S.M.C., Copyright © 1994 by Richard G. Lawrence, and reprinted by permission of the artist. Artwork on the half-title page, "Father, Son, Soldier, and Marine," Copyright © 1994 by Richard G. Lawrence, and reprinted by permission of the artist.

"Backfire" first appeared in IKON #7 (1987), Copyright © 1984 by Mary Moran. Reprinted by permission of the author.

Grateful acknowledgment is made for permission to print excerpts from "Cracks In the Wall," Copyright © 1992 by Clarence E. Orr, and reprinted by permission of the author.

Grateful acknowledgment is made for permission to print "Leading All the Way," Copyright © 1993, and "A Soldier Returns Home," Copyright © 1987 by Gregory Schlieve, and reprinted by permission of the author.

Grateful acknowledgment is made for permission to publish the art of Ralph Sirianni, Copyright © 1993 by Ralph Sirianni, and reprinted by permission of the artist.

Artwork on the cover, Copyright © 1993 by Ralph Sirianni, and reprinted by permission of the artist.

Grateful acknowledgment is made for permission to print excerpts from "Fire In the Hole," Copyright © 1991 by Dennis R. Tenety, and reprinted by permission of the author.

Grateful acknowledgment is made for permission to print the poetry of Walter Vieira, Copyright © 1994 by Walter Vieira, and reprinted by permission of the author.

International Standard Book Number: 0-9629164-6-3
Library of Congress Catalogue Card Number: 94-69895
Printed in the United States of America

To Barbara, with love

CONTENTS

About the Editors

Sarah B. Hansel conceived the project to develop *Soldier's Heart.* She received her Doctorate in Clinical Psychology from Southern Illinois University in 1986 and has worked in the treatment of trauma originating from combat and from child abuse as well as sexual assault. She is a member of the Trauma Recovery Service Team at Perry Point VA Medical Center and volunteers at the Domestic Violence/Rape Crisis Center in Elkton, MD.

Ann Steidle earned her Master's degree in Adult Psychiatric and Mental Health Nursing at the University of Maryland. She has worked as a team member in Perry Point's Trauma Recovery Service, and as a Clinical Specialist in VA Medical Centers. She consults as a private practitioner in the areas of pregnancy and addiction at University of Maryland Hospital.

Grace Zaczek, president of the National Trauma Institute at Baltimore, earned her Bachelor's degree in Nursing at Columbia University and a Master's of Public Health at the Johns Hopkins University. She works as a Community Health Nurse Coordinator in Delaware and has chaired several health planning committees in Maryland. A volunteer in the Vet Center Outreach Program, she has shared her experience in living with a veteran with PTSD with family members in treatment.

Ron Zaczek, principal editor of *Soldier's Heart,* flew 393 combat missions as a helicopter crewchief with Marine Observation Squadron 3 (VMO-3) in Phu Bai, Vietnam in 1967, earning 19 Air Medals and the Bronze Star. He was awarded a Bachelor's degree in Engineering from the University of Maryland. Diagnosed with PTSD in 1981, he received therapy in the Vet Center program. His 1994 book, *Farewell, Darkness: A Veteran's Triumph over Combat Trauma* (Naval Institute Press), captures his wartime and treatment experiences.

About the National Trauma Institute at Baltimore, Inc.

The NTIB is a non-profit organization whose objectives are to support and encourage research on treatment for individuals diagnosed with psychological trauma disorders; support and encourage education for individuals having such disorders, and their families; and publish and distribute materials which enhance knowledge of psychological trauma disorders and their treatment. The governing board is composed of clinicians specializing in treating traumatic disorders, individuals diagnosed with such disorders, and family members of such individuals.

ACKNOWLEDGMENTS

The editors wish to thank the following people for their expertise, time, and invaluable support.

Most of all, we thank the veterans, family members, and treatment professionals who shared often painful expressions of their experience surviving combat trauma so that the road others travel is made less lonely.

It is impossible to measure the thanks owed to Dr. Thomas Murtaugh, who provided insight, guided us to resources, gave his generous support, and finally, cooked some extraordinary meals to nourish us all in this project.

Special thanks to Esther Giller, president of the Sidran Foundation, for her confidence, guidance, and support throughout all phases of this project, and Mary Medland of Sidran Press for aggressively pursuing all avenues to obtain submissions.

Thanks to the many Vet Centers and to the Specialized Inpatient PTSD Units that made the request for submissions available to their clients, and to the following individuals and organizations: Susan Roth and Mary Beth Williams of the International Society for Traumatic Stress Studies; Linda Schwartz of the Vietnam Veterans of America and the staff of the VVA Veteran ; Gregory A. Offringa, L.I.C.S.W. for the introductory essay on PTSD which accompanied our request for submissions; SSgt. Randall Lusk for lists of organizations that could help. Thanks to all the military organizations that assisted in distributing our request for submissions through their newsletters, especially: the Vietnam Helicopter Crew Members Association, International

(Wayne Mutza and Spencer Gardner); "The Marine Corps Gazette," The Americal Division Association; USMC Vietnam Helicopter Pilots and Aircrew Reunion; 1st Cavalry Division Association; 1st Marine Aircraft Wing Association; Jewish War Veterans of the U.S.A.; and the Military Order of the Cootie.

Special thanks to Ralph Sirianni for his haunting cover image. Thanks to designer Alan Carter for pulling words and art together in an attractive volume.

Thanks to the following individuals for help and guidance in building our non-profit organization: William Price II, Esq. for assistance in incorporation; Thomas Marshall Brooks for teaching us accounting skills; John Wheeler Glenn, Esq. for providing our initial meeting places.

Thanks to Barbara Bill, Christopher and Matthew Zaczek, and John McCook for assistance in preparing and distributing the calls for submission. Thanks to Lisa Holden and Yvonne St. George for help in preparing the manuscript and other clerical tasks. Thanks to Dr. Pat Fox and Joan Dixon for reviewing the manuscript.

". . . Had (he) been a veteran of the Civil War, the doctors would have called his malady 'Soldiers Heart.' Had he served in World War I, they would have said he suffered from 'Shell Shock.' After World War II and Korea, they would have labeled him with 'Combat Fatigue' or 'Nerves.' Since . . . Vietnam, modern psychiatry has given the illness a name drained of both poetry and blame—Post Traumatic Stress Disorder."

" 'Soldiers Heart' though, remains a pretty good name for it, for PTSD is a disorder of warriors, not men and women who were weak or cowardly, but to the contrary, a disorder of those who followed orders and who at a young age put their feelings aside and performed unimaginable tasks that most human beings never encounter. PTSD is a disorder of the good warrior."

Anonymous
From "Sharing the Struggles of a Friend" by George Hill, U.S.M.C., disabled veteran. Originally appeared in *The Gainesville Sun*, November 10, 1993. Reprinted by permission.

INTRODUCTION

About Post Traumatic Stress Disorder

Every civilization has known that going into combat changes the person who fights. History has recorded many names for the syndrome currently identified as Post-Traumatic Stress Disorder. After each conflict there is an awareness that those who return from war suffer in similar ways, having nightmares, thinking obsessively of their war experiences, and feeling anger and depression. In the aftermath of America's Civil War, the condition was known as Soldier's Heart. During the first World War, there was a belief that the changes in air pressure created by exploding bombs caused physical harm to the nerves and the problem became known as Shell Shock.[1] In World War II, it was learned that "breakdown" could occur in anyone who was in battle long enough. The new label became Combat Fatigue.[2] Since 1980, when the American Psychiatric Association published the Diagnostic and Statistical Manual of Mental Disorders (DSM-III), the name Post-Traumatic Stress Disorder (PTSD) has been the official diagnosis for the physical and psychological effects of overwhelming events such as those survived by combat veterans. These manuals, the most current being DSM-IV[3], are designed to help distinguish among all the possible psychiatric diagnoses. They provide rules or guidelines, which are the defining characteristics of a disorder including PTSD.

Anyone can develop PTSD. The magnitude of the trauma survived by the person is more important in developing PTSD than the initial strength or psychological fitness of the survivor. Aphrodite Matsakis illustrates this with the example of accidentally cutting your finger with a knife.[4] If the blade is sharp and the force is great enough, you could lose part of your finger. The degree of injury depends "more on the sharpness of the blade and power behind it, than on the toughness of your skin." With enough force, even the world's toughest skin will be cut. The same is true in developing PTSD. DSM-IV defines the "trauma" causing PTSD as an event in which the person experiences, witnesses, or confronts actual or threatened death, or serious injury to self or others. The person responds with fear, helplessness, or horror—the common feelings of combat. Soldiers are wounded, they see trusted comrades "blown away" while they are unable to do anything to prevent or change what has happened.

Even though people try to put upsetting experiences "in the past" and forget them, traumatic memories come back in a variety of ways. During the day, there may be recurrent recollections of the event which feel intrusive, like a song that you can't get out of your mind. At night, there may be repeating dreams and nightmares about what happened during the war. Vets can feel intense anxiety when exposed to reminders that resemble the original trauma. These triggers may be external—a passing helicopter, the backfire of an automobile, bursting fireworks. Other triggers are internal, such as having a feeling similar to the way the person felt during or preceding the traumatic event. Sometimes, veterans act or feel as if the event itself were re-occurring. These "flashbacks" can range from a dim sense of being in two places at one time (the "here and now," as well as "back then") to becoming totally immersed in the intruding memory, losing track of place and time. Flashbacks are sometimes terrifying, but may occasionally be pleasurable when they recall a time the veteran felt in control and powerful. Often, the memory of the event is fragmented. Important parts are lost to recall, and the connection between the veteran's feelings of anxiety, dreams, or flashbacks and a specific trigger may not be obvious. The vet senses only that something is wrong, and doesn't connect it to a specific wartime experience, or indeed, to his or her combat history at all.

When people experience a traumatic event, a conflict is set up in the mind between the need to acknowledge and bear witness to the event, and the desire to forget or deny the event ever took place.[5] The effort to deny provides the energy that creates a set of symptoms that DSM-IV describes as the "persistent avoidance of things associated with the trauma." This is accompanied by a general numbing of re-

sponsiveness that was not part of the person's character before the traumatic event. Survivors will try to avoid thinking or talking about things
that bring the trauma to mind. They may give curt answers to questions
about combat to keep people from asking any more. They may avoid
activities or places that arouse memories. For example, not reading
books or going to movies about the conflict in which he or she served.
Because many of the reminders are part of everyday life, this avoidance can restrict survivors' enjoyment of life and begin to constrict
their daily routine. A vet may not attend the annual Fourth of July celebration because fireworks make him uncomfortable. The vet may
prevent his or her family from attending the celebration as well. Such
restrictions prevent the entire family from "having fun" and can lead
to damaged relationships with friends, resentment between spouses,
and children who feel denied the opportunity to "do what the other
kids do."

Veteran's feelings may be restricted; he or she may not be able to
get in touch with strong emotions such as love. This heightens a sense
of detachment and being different from others, a sense of isolation, and
"not being able to feel." Along with these symptoms, survivors may
have a foreshortened sense of the future. They don't believe that they
will live very long, and it becomes difficult for them to plan for life
events such as marriage and retirement. Avoiding things that remind
them of their traumatic experiences and avoiding planning for the future cause vets to miss many life experiences which present opportuni-
ties that could diminish the effect of the trauma and enable them to successfully cope with their experience.[6]

Normally, people react to threat with a series of changes in
arousal and attention. When aroused, the sympathetic nervous system
sets up the bodily changes associated with the "flight or fight" response. Adrenaline rushes through the body and attention becomes focused on the source of the perceived threat. The normal perceptions of
pain, hunger, or fatigue are dampened and the body is ready to protect
itself. There may be intense feelings of fear or anger. All these changes
are the natural way the human body is designed to respond to danger.
These changes have survival value, allowing the person to run away
and escape, or turn and face the danger. With PTSD, changes that are
part of the "flight or fight" response can persist long after the danger
has passed. The body continues to react as if immediately threatened,
making it difficult to fall asleep, or sleep through the entire night.
Trauma survivors are often hyper-aware of their environment, con-

stantly scanning for signs of threat. They may be easily startled and have trouble concentrating. Frequent irritability, with sudden outbursts of anger, are also hallmarks of PTSD.

The symptoms of intrusion and avoidance alternate over time: sometimes a person is overwhelmed with memories of the trauma, often responding with intense feelings. At other times, he will be distant, icily calm, and avoid anything that could remind him of the trauma. However, the symptoms that indicate increased arousal are persistent and may be interpreted by others as part of the survivor's personality, rather than recognized as part of the disorder.

The intensity of the symptoms will vary and the problems of PTSD may be disguised by addictive or compulsive behaviors, such as alcoholism, drug abuse, eating disorders, and workaholism. Trauma survivors engage in these behaviors to avoid thinking about their experiences.

As human beings grow and mature, we develop a set of basic assumptions about the world and our place in it. These serve as our operating rules and are so deep inside that we don't even think about them. The most central assumptions are a sense of safety and basic trust in our fellow man. This develops from our earliest relationship with our caregivers and allows us to relate to other people. Most of us grow up believing the world is benevolent and meaningful, and ourselves to be essentially good individuals. Trauma has a profound effect on these assumptions, as well as the individuals' sense of being in control. When our assumptions about the world are shattered, so are our means of connecting with others. Relationships within the family, the community, and religion are all vulnerable to the changes an individual experiences in trauma.

The basic task of healing from trauma is for survivors to reconnect with themselves, with their families, and society. This is accomplished by developing a new perspective, one that allows people to make sense of the traumatic experience and allows them to regain a sense of control. This new perspective is created by developing a relationship with another person. For many, that relationship is in therapy, however therapy is not the only relationship in which healing can occur. Healing can take place with the aid of a supportive spouse, family, friends, or minister—relationships where the veteran feels in charge of the process and can trust the other person enough to risk looking at the traumatic experience, remembering what happened, putting it into context and filling in any gaps. To do this, survivors must be able to tolerate arousal and strong, distressing emotions. Finally, the trauma survivor must accept himself or herself, which occurs in part through being accepted by another.

The role of other people in the healing process is crucial. As with all truly powerful things, the responses of other people can harm as well as help. Negative responses such as stigmatizing and blaming the victim or minimizing the experience can be devastating to trauma survivors and their families. Helpful responses include those which demonstrate acceptance of the person, genuine concern, empathy, willingness to listen, and respect.

Defining the disorder is easier than defining healing or recovery. The trauma can never be erased. The survivor has lived through an experience and has been changed by it. Recovery might be better understood as a return to effective functioning. One formula suggested for psychological well-being includes: being involved in the present and hopeful about the future; being capable of feeling pleasure; being free of very disturbing thoughts or feelings; and being able to maintain meaningful relationships.[7] These are reasonable goals for trauma survivors.

The movement from trauma to effective functioning is a challenging path that has qualities unique to each person who embarks upon the journey. The experiences of veterans who have written for this book show the common elements of dealing with PTSD. The courage and feeling demonstrated by each author, artist, and poet touch universal truths known to all who have experienced PTSD, and we hope will help shed some light on the path for others to follow. More detailed information on PTSD and the recovery process is available in some of the books in the Resource Guide.

Notes

1. James Goodwin, *The Etiology of Combat-Related Post-Traumatic Stress Disorder* (Cincinnati: Disabled American Veterans, 1980), 5.
2. J.W. Appel and G.W. Beebe, quoted in Judith Herman, *Trauma and Recovery* (New York: Basic Books, 1992), 25.
3. American Psychiatric Association, *Diagnostic and Statistical Manual of Mental Disorders,* 4th ed. (Washington, D.C.: American Psychiatric Press, 1994).
4. Aphrodite Matsakis, *I Can't Get Over It: A Handbook for Survivors of Trauma* (Oakland: New Harbinger Publications, Inc., 1992).
5. Appel and Beebe, quoted in Herman, 1.

6. Ibid., 47.
7. Ronni Janoff-Bulman, *Shattered Assumptions: Toward a New Psychology of Trauma* (New York: The Free Press, 1992), 11.

How to Use This Book

This book is intended for use by anyone who is a survivor of combat or who cares about such a veteran. Spouses, therapists, friends, families, and those who would like to understand—from the veteran's point of view—what the long-term consequences of combat can be are invited to read and share the words of those who live the experience.

Veterans—
- may find comfort in knowing they are not alone
- may find words for what they could not express
- may recognize their healing journey in the words of others
- may be inspired to use positive coping skills, such as journal writing and talking to others
- may take hope

Clinicians—
- may have a tool to share with veterans
- may be sensitized to the issues of combat vets
- may use this book as a springboard for discussion
- may recognize themselves

Spouses, families, and friends—
- may gain insight into the complex, painful, and often frightening world of those they love
- may understand more about the disorder to encourage their friend or partner to get treatment
- may find reassurance that others in similar situations are prevailing

About This Book

Since the end of World War II, a substantial body of literature has been written on the causes and treatment of war-related traumatic stress disorder. Why, then, another book on combat trauma? What contribution does *Soldier's Heart* make to veterans, their families, and treatment professionals? How is it different from other books?

Most literature that addresses combat trauma is written by or for treatment professionals, and is not widely read by vets. Most veteran writings are in the nature of "war stories," which capture the actual combat experience, but not the emotional legacy of trauma, its effect on their lives, or upon their families. Although treatment processes have been recorded in exacting detail by clinicians, few vets write of seeking help and fewer still have written of their experience in therapy for combat trauma, a deeply personal and sensitive issue that is difficult to share with others.

In war, soldiers, sailors, airmen, and Marines quickly learn to count on each other for survival. Vets often don't believe that anyone, including family and treatment professionals, who hasn't endured combat can understand or help them deal with the effects of combat trauma. Veterans often have difficulty describing their experiences and feelings to family and friends. Family members frequently don't know how to respond in ways the veteran will accept. The editors, a team of clinicians, a veteran recovered from PTSD, and his spouse, recognized the need for a book written by veterans and family members, for vets and their families, that would help survivors—veteran and family alike—cope with the effects of combat trauma in their lives.

Working as a team, clinicians Sarah Hansel and Ann Steidle, Marine Vietnam veteran Ron Zaczek, and his wife Grace Zaczek formed a non-profit organization, The National Trauma Institute at Baltimore, whose mission is to advocate for those experiencing stress related traumas, their families, and clinicians working with these individuals. The Institute's first project is *Soldier's Heart,* a collective work on combat-induced traumatic stress disorder.

We saw in *Soldier's Heart* a means of letting veterans and families step back from the stress with which they live, take stock of where they are, and articulate their feelings. Sidran Press' successful experience in producing a collective work on multiple personality disorder, *Multiple Personality Disorder From the Inside Out,* provided a roadmap to guide our project.

The primary challenges were to obtain submissions of essays, art, and poetry from veterans and family members, and then organize the material in a logical, easily read format. We produced a "Call for Submissions" that described the project, its benefits, and presented guidelines to assist authors in framing their response:

- What having PTSD, Shell Shock, or Battle Fatigue means to you and to your family
- How combat trauma makes you feel, how it makes you see your world
- What you wished you knew about combat trauma when you were first diagnosed
- The most helpful aspects of therapy or the healing experience
- What you think family members should know
- For family members: What would you like to share from your experience with a loved one or friend suffering from combat trauma? How you coped

Nearly 6,000 submission forms were direct-mailed to the Department of Veterans Affairs' Veterans Outreach Centers and In-Patient PTSD Units. Public service advertisements in veteran publications such as the Vietnam Veterans of America's "Veteran," and military unit newsletters, along with word-of-mouth publicity by individual veterans, their families, and clinicians generated a wide response. Submission forms were also distributed at the Vietnam Veterans' Memorial during the tenth anniversary celebration of its dedication and at the dedication of the Vietnam Women's Memorial.

Two hundred submissions were received from more than 70 authors. The echoes of war reverberated from Bougainville, Leyte, and Iwo Jima, on to Taegu, down the years to the Mekong Delta and Khe Sanh, then to Beirut, and the Saudi Arabian desert. Whether known as PTSD, battle fatigue, nerves, or, as one W.W. II veteran wrote in an accompanying letter "having shit in your blood," veterans of World War II, Korea, Vietnam, Lebanon, Grenada, Panama, and Desert Storm describe feelings and experiences common to vets of all wars.

During the submission process, great care was taken to protect authors' and artists' confidentiality, stating that individuals would be identified as "John, D., Sgt., U.S. Army," "J.S., nurse, Vietnam," or anonymously. However, many authors expressed a strong desire to be identified with their work, and are identified as they requested. Our editorial policy was to maintain the original "voice" of the author. Some submissions were edited for clarity and to excerpt the most pertinent passages, while preserving the author's meaning. A major objective was to use at least one submission from each contributor. Nearly every author or artist who provided material is represented in the final work.

In a few cases, submissions were not used because they recounted a combat incident, rather than the impact of combat on the veteran's life.

During the preliminary editing of the contributions, it became clear that the information elicited by the "Call for Submissions" was much broader than anticipated and organizing the book presented a significant challenge. We had anticipated straightforward responses to our questions from vets who had survived combat trauma. We received, instead, an emotional outpouring of eloquent and compelling prose, poetry, and art that covered the range of experiences across time of veterans and their families living with PTSD. The result is a book far more powerful than anything we had anticipated; it is quite literally a moving picture of the full range of combat trauma from emerging awareness, through grief and despair, to acceptance and hope. The collected writings illustrate how an individual can and did change across time, with the work of several veterans appearing in different chapters throughout the book.

Male and female veterans alike wrote eloquently of their ordeals. Husbands and wives expressed their desire to understand and help their veteran spouse. We heard from veterans living successful professional lives and those in prison, veterans moving frequently to escape their anger, families torn apart by PTSD, spouses waiting patiently for their veteran to reach out for help, counselors trying to understand, and friends who supported the veterans in war and still care for them.

The editors had no preconceived structure for the book; we looked to the vet's writings to give it form. *Stress and Frustration* by Irving L. Janis, Ph.D., was a source of inspiration in defining the chapters.[1] The submissions touched us on many levels, including an emotional one. Common threads began to emerge as we worked to organize the contributions. Many submissions carried several threads, and could have been placed in more than one chapter. In these cases, we selected the dominant theme and have presented the work in a way that best preserves the author's intent. The organization of the book is not intended to reflect a model for war-related stress disorders or a treatment process, but recognizes the common themes that veterans and their families express.

The writings in the first chapter share a common thread in their expression of the raw symptoms of combat trauma such as fury, isolation, flashbacks, nightmares, emotional numbing—a sense of being out of control. Authors display varying degrees of recognition of how their symptoms stem from wartime experience. Some connect their symptoms to a specific combat incident, often through a flashback or an intruding memory. Others give voice to an unfocused, baffled fury as their feelings overwhelm them, knowing only that something is wrong and shouting, "I hurt!"

The common theme in the second chapter is isolation, stemming from the rejection the veteran feels from the nation, family, and former friends as well as the veteran's own rejection of "the system" because of what it has done to him or her.

The third chapter centers on veterans' attempts to find help, sometimes successfully, and sometimes in vain. In vets' eyes the quality of professional treatment is unreliable. Veterans' comments about the therapeutic process, about "good" and "bad" therapists, the pitfalls and benefits of the in-patient and Vet Center environments, and the use of drug therapy are valuable learning tools for professionals and lay readers alike. Clinicians also describe the effect of treatment on veterans, and on themselves.

The theme of Chapter Four is despair, the loss of the bright future veterans had expected; frustration with their present lives, and anger at how they are not the people they'd hoped to be.

Chapter Five shows the deep sorrow of comrades, families, and friends for those lost in combat. These writings illustrate the movement from grief to remembrance and a spiritual acceptance of the loss.

In Chapter Six, veterans tell of their attempts to escape pain and anger through frequent job changes, drug use, and alcohol. Even so, authors display the courage that enables them to come back and face the feelings from which they tried to flee.

Family and friends write in Chapter Seven of the impact of combat trauma on the lives of those they love, and in turn, on themselves. Deep support and love alternate with impatience and hostility at the veteran's sometimes baffling behavior. Those who carry the memory of veterans who did not return, POWs and MIAs, write of lives "caught between yesterday and tomorrow."

In the final chapter, the unifying thread is the veterans' need to "make sense out of it all," strongly supported by a growing awareness that they are regaining control of their lives. Some accommodate their lives to the burdens of trauma they know they continue to carry. They view this burden as their legacy, but function successfully in society in spite of memories that still haunt them. Others find ways to lay down their burden. They write of accepting the death of friends, of finishing grieving. They accept the impact of their combat experience and write of forgiving themselves for the things they have done, or did not do, and of finding ways to be happy. In some veterans, this acceptance evolves to a feeling of peace as healing from trauma enables them to rejoin the world of work, play, and love.

Readers suffering from combat trauma and their families will undoubtedly search for themselves in these pages. We hope that they will benefit from the sense of brotherhood and community they find—that they will see they are not alone and can prevail, and that the wisdom in this collective voice will help them find peace.

The National Trauma Institute at Baltimore
October 1994

Note
1. Irving L. Janis, *Stress and Frustration* (New York: Harcourt Brace Jovanovitch, 1969).

PROLOGUE: A SURVIVOR'S VIEW

Ann Powlas
1st Lieutenant, USA Nurse Corps,
3rd Field Hospital Vietnam, 1971-1972

PTSD means anger, shame, isolation, guilt, nightmares, pain, numbing, and praying for death.

I didn't know why I was suddenly so angry or how to express my anger. The feelings had been pushed down too long and there was an explosion. The anger made me strike out at whatever was nearest, which sometimes was my own body or that of someone dear to me. The explosion was a release, but then there was the shame and guilt about how I had released it. A person has to be crazy to cut, stab, or poison herself. I couldn't let anyone know because of the shame. How could anyone else understand when I didn't? I just knew the anger couldn't be pushed down anymore. I withdrew from people or wore a mask when I was with them. If they really knew me, they would see the shame and know there was something terribly wrong with me.

It couldn't be PTSD because I was just a female nurse in Vietnam. Nurses are strong and always take care of others. Females aren't in combat in the bush. We had cots, hot food, and showers, and we were in a hospital. If there was something wrong with me, it was my fault because I was weak. Women aren't supposed to know what war is like. You mean it isn't like John Wayne, where only the bad guy gets hurt and the good guy comes home a hero? Women don't die in war zones, but look at the young nurses on the "Wall." I wish I didn't know war destroys everyone it touches. The ones that die quickly are lucky. They can't remember all the kids at the orphanages who came running to us for hugs and attention—just someone to care about them. Remember when one of those little boys came running to us with a piece of metal in his eye? His eye was protruding from its socket. I never saw him again except in my mind with that eye protruding and his smile. Remember the rows of babies lying in their own waste with flies swarming all around them? Their eyes were blank; too weak to cry; arms and legs pencil thin; and their bellies so swollen, they looked as if they would explode. There were not enough nuns to care for them or to even hold them. Remember the street kids who were thieves or pimps just to survive? The boys sold their sisters so the family could have shelter and rice. Remember the old men and women who have never seen peace? Their homes and families destroyed again and again. Their eyes are blank and they don't smile. Peace comes only with death.

Remember our teenage patients suffering through horrible fevers and wounds beyond imagination? I tell some they will be okay and then they die. Death is peace, but yet they never lived. They will never play again, make love, have a family, or face a challenging career. There is only a grieving girlfriend, wife, or parent left. Another body bag because of the political or financial ambition of someone in power. They say he or she died for freedom, but I don't see it. For hospital staff, there is guilt over what was or wasn't done. Don't feel it. Just do your job. When the job is done, drown it all with alcohol. There is no guilt, no tears, no sadness, and no distrust of the government; but there is also no joy, no peace nor love. I existed.

After days, months, and years, the numbing doesn't work anymore. There has to be more to life than this. The emotional pain is worse than any physical pain. I tried counselors, but they told me "You should be happy," "forget Vietnam, it is over," and "what do you want?" I knew there was something terribly wrong with me, I was hopeless and full of shame. The wound deepened, eating me alive. I cried and prayed to God to please just let me die. I finally met a counselor who cared, but she had to move, leaving my husband and me alone again in this nightmare. Barry cared, but couldn't understand what was going on. I was afraid he would leave me.

Desert Storm started and I couldn't stand the thought of more wasted lives. I couldn't stand to see the terror in the eyes of a reporter during a missile attack. My own terror was still with me. I had a friend struggling, along with my husband, to keep me alive. I would try a therapist one more time for them, but I knew it wouldn't help. I took that risk and found someone who listened and didn't judge me, but I knew it wouldn't last. I would get close to someone, then he or she would die or move on. As time went by, she didn't leave and there were others willing to go through the pain with me.

As months and years went by, I gradually felt peace and joy. There is still pain that I want to drown, instead I make a phone call. There is still guilt for not being the perfect nurse at 21, but I'm starting to feel some compassion for that young woman who thought she could save the world. I still feel shame when I tell someone I have retired. They say I'm too young to retire. I feel very old. If I say I have PTSD, they don't understand. I feel I'm a burden on society because I'm no longer a productive citizen. The stress of a job is too much and my mind doesn't function as I think it should. I can't comprehend or remember the simplest things. My choices in life are down to those things that aren't triggers, which makes me angry. I feel like a rebellious child who has been told "no."

After almost three years, I am still on medication, see a therapist, attend a 12-Step Group, and still need reassurance that I won't be left alone. It takes all of them to help me cope with everyday life. Now I also have the Vietnam Women's Memorial to help carry some of the burden. I have placed my life in God's hands and try to live just each moment. One day, I would like to wake up from this nightmare and find I'm a "normal" person, instead of a disabled burden on society. I'm extremely grateful for my husband and others who struggle through this nightmare with me.

1

SOMETHING'S WRONG

"The soul remembers what the heart disavows: being mortally
wounded by each soldier who died."
Dana S.

As veterans become aware that there has been no true return from the
war, and that their "problems" may be related to their combat experience, their writings reflect the raw symptoms of combat trauma. Memories and feelings are recorded in baffled fury, capturing a sense of being apart and different. The rushing memories are often fragmented,
like clips from a movie, or slides from a carousel—difficult to grasp
and to face. Some lead to flashbacks in the day, others fuel the night
horrors. These are some of the intrusive symptoms of combat trauma.
As remembering grows more painful, defense mechanisms kick in and
vets write of amnesia, loss of feeling, loneliness, and isolation. These
are the numbing symptoms of PTSD.

Healing from PTSD is a process of making connections, but what
seems obvious to family members or to therapists, is not so obvious to
veterans, who struggle against feelings they may neither understand

nor connect to their combat experience. The views recorded in the essays and poetry in this chapter begin as *feelings* to the veterans who live them. These feelings influence veterans' actions and how they deal with other people. They feel rage, distrust, loneliness, or depression. At other times vets feel like they can't feel at all, and act remote and distant to both loved ones and friends. The vet begins to recognize that these feelings and actions may be symptoms of combat trauma, only after he or she begins to make connections between current life and prior combat experience. Before he or she can make these connections, a vet must admit, often grudgingly, and often at the insistence of spouse or family, that "something is wrong." Veterans who contributed to this book did so as survivors of combat trauma, and so there is an implicit awareness in the writings that follow that something is wrong, and that it is connected to the war. Usually, professional help is required before the vet begins to recognize that the cause of his or her problems lies "in the war."

In the past decade, vets have been inundated with information about PTSD, and those who live with it know there is no shame to the disorder. Nevertheless, as a vet becomes more and more aware that something is wrong in his or her life, there is a strong tendency to deny both the feelings, and their connection to the war. Vets may suspect they are suffering from the effects of combat, or they may deny it, but as the feelings intensify, the one thing that the vet knows, and fears, is loss of control. The sense of losing control is terrifying. In combat, survival—for the vet, and for the team— meant staying in control. Loss of control was, and remains, unthinkable, and to the veteran is a sign of weakness and shame. Vets may feel too proud or too stubborn, to "admit weakness" by asking for help from others, or they may not want it. As their feelings mount, few will recognize that their actions and feelings are symptoms of combat trauma; they are only aware, and certain, that they hurt. Often, it falls to loved ones and friends to make the first move towards seeking help as the vet displays increasing symptoms of combat trauma.

A word of caution is advised in reading this book, particularly the material in this chapter. The symptoms of intrusion and numbing extend with varying degrees of intensity throughout a survivor's life with PTSD. The writings in this chapter are the kinds of shrill cries, flashes of rage, and silent, embarrassed fears that vets demonstrate at the dinner table, in tension-filled conversations with friends and co-workers, by themselves in a mall, or when they desperately seek help at a treatment facility for the first time. While the essays and poetry that follow demonstrate feelings or actions that may, for each individual, be symptoms of combat trauma, the reader is cautioned against attempting self-diagnosis. Identifying with "one numbing" and "three intrusions" in the following pages is not a diagnosis of PTSD, but may be a sign that professional help is needed.

INTRUSION

After surviving a terrible event, veterans often find that they are unable to put the experience to rest. They may become overwhelmed by the same intense feelings which their experience has engendered. These feelings come upon them without provocation, or explode inside when confronted with reminders. Sometimes the same feeling expressed in a minor key will call forth the intense eruptions of fear, anger, or sadness that are the survivor's legacy.

Sometimes the event returns as memory, but of such vividness that veterans actually "see" the event over and over again and feel immersed in it. This experience has come to be called "flashbacks." Alternatively, the memories intrude upon a veteran's sleep, creating nightmares that awaken him or her with their power, or cause them to sleep restlessly. These nightmares, known as Combat Dreams, sometimes make vets dread sleeping.

The memories can be fragmented; pictures without sounds, sensations without pictures. Brief snatches of reality, often unconnected, can occur, which frightens veterans and fills them with foreboding.

This process can intensify the sense of difference which most vets already feel. Not only have they experienced things that members of the safe, civilian world have not, but they are unable to let go of them. A realization gradually dawns that the veteran has not yet been released from an event, now distant in place and time. This difference creates a sense of alienation towards the people who now surround him. Tragically, this leaves victims of combat trauma further alone with their memories.

Moore, No More

Walter "Angus" Vieira
Corporal, USMC, SLF 9th MAB RLT 26 5th Marines,
Vietnam, 1967

You Bastard!
You Whore!
You killed my friend,
Moore.

"Y-Y, You know, Angus"
He'd stutter with a
smile.

A smile that gave me strength
to go that extra, big
mile.

A shiny black
face
and not so very tall.
A guy who blended in,
you wouldn't notice him
at all.

He didn't die no special
way,
like charging a hill.
Just walking in
column,
you picked him out, my good
friend Moore, you shot to
kill.

I heard you fire
that single round.
Seemed too far off for us to
dread.

I just kept walking
til' I got to the spot.
My good buddy
Moore, lay dead.

What made you choose
him?
This little black
kid.
No more than
eighteen.
Who stuttered
and smiled,
whose only real
wish
was to be
a Marine.

This kid wouldn't hurt
you.
I know it for sure.
He told me in secret
He fired high.

It's me that you wanted.
I'd slice your throat
gladly
and that you can bet is no
lie.

But isn't that the
way
In this thing
they call war?
The innocent fall
to the floor.
That's the only real
reason
you *had* to go and do
it

You no good; you Bastard!
You Whore!

You *had* to go and kill
him.
You just couldn't leave
him.
My great little buddy,
named
Moore.

"Y-Y, You know, Angus, You know."

Survivors of Combat Trauma!

David H.
USA, Americal Division, Vietnam

I died back in Nam in '68, a little at a time, when we came back from the leech hole. We didn't know that people, especially our own family, would reject us.

Talk about "PTSD," well let me tell ya, those of us, especially from the bush, suffer some kind of it. I haven't found one vet yet who doesn't. The way I feel is, life has no f . . . . g meaning here on earth anyway. I'm from a large family, five brothers and three sisters, if I can still call 'em family! It's obvious they don't need me but I say, "F—— em!" Who cares what I went through and am still going through? I got seriously wounded in Nam. My chest was blown right out by an AK-47. Put me in a hospital the first time for about 15 months. Before they got me I remember one big firefight. When it was over, there were only two men left in my squad. My sergeant, who only had two weeks to go before he was to go home, was killed. Yes, he was my best friend. That's when I lost it. When it was over I had to drag him by rope when we policed up the dead and wounded.

When I got home I got into the drugs, alcohol, etc. I was on a sui-cide mission and still am. I'm not into the drugs as much or alcohol but ending my life still stands. I live my life as a loner, going through depression, pain, and the whole ball of wax. I've lost most of my money. I've tried everything to fit in society. It doesn't work!

I've been married 24 years and in my first 12 years of marriage I've moved over 57 times, dragged my family all around the U.S. We have two children and they, too, are having problems. People that never had to experience the shit we did will never understand. Today it's even worse. Take a look around. People aren't human anymore—all they think about are themselves. They don't know what it's like to walk by simple things like a flower. Pick it up, smell it, and feel for what it really is, like we would. No, they'd more likely step on it and walk on by. There was a saying, "It's not what we can do for ourselves, but what for our country." Shit, it's taking care of ya own ass today just trying to survive. Sometimes, I wish I could go back to Nam. I'd kill every f . . . . g thing in sight! This crap never ends. It's only over when it's over. Ask yourselves a question, look around, and see what our world is doing and then say, "For what?"

I'm gonna find myself some land, cast the world out, dig my hole, and live in it. When they bury me, make sure they shine my ass and stick it upward and out of the ground. When someone walks by they can just squat down and kiss the brown spot!

Well, I'm signing off, cause anger can just go on and on. When you see this you'll probably say yeah just another one, a screwed up, but I say who f . . . g cares?

Anyway—You! Have a good day.

Call me "Leech," US Army, Vietnam

Clyde Q.
Corporal, USMC (R), South Korea, 1950–1951

What hurts the most is that many younger people of this generation do not understand why I break into tears when I have read or seen something to bring back emotional memories of the Korean War.

I see something sad on TV and I start sobbing. I have to leave the room to spare myself embarrassment in front of friends and family. How do I explain to visitors who do not know of my condition . . . why I am crying?

Sometimes I feel less than a man when I cry. Nine years of active service in the Marine Corps . . . and I cry. A 64-year-old man who cries . . . I feel depressed and at times angry.

PTSD and the Ho Bo Woods

Larry Young
Specialist/5, USA, Combat Medic,
25th Inf Div, Vietnam, 1969

Life is a minefield,
one wrong step to death,
or a booby-trap grenade
exploding!

My self-image shattered.
My personality fractured.
Rage is the explosive!
Fragmented, I try picking
up the pieces.

Of Recent Death

Kellan Kyllo
USMC, HMM-162, Ky Ha, Marble Mountain,
Quang Tri, Vietnam, 1966-1968

Down the center of a long
dark corridor
he walked slowly,
quietly,
arms tightened against his sides,
a
dead friend
reached through the wall,
grabbed,
almost got him.

4th of July

Ken Sauvage
Corporal, USMC, 2nd Bn 3rd Marines,
Vietnam, 1968-1969

Watching the parade
standing in the hot sun
remembering other hot suns
other men who once marched.
On this gentle July evening
rifle fire in the twilight
machine guns ripping flesh
colors stain the dark sky.

Iwo Jima

Charles Felix
Corporal, USMC, W.W. II:
Bougainville, Guam, Iwo Jima

Brooding, sullen, inscrutable Iwo.
Amid your sifting ashes there still lie
The rusting relics of a savage foe,
And the memories of bravery that never die.

Bleak broke the dreadful day.
When Hell opened its dripping maw
And death's suffocating sweet decay,
Wafted amid dreadful sights that youthful warriors saw.

And you, craggy, towering Suribachi,
Will ever time erase?
The nightmare journey on hand and knee,
Across the pitted inferno of your face.

You came to know death well that day.
As your caves rocked with grenade
Gave up their bleating, cornered prey,
To the flame-throwers searing, charring accolade.

Do you recall in murky pall the flash?
On bayonet as young men rose to fight.
And heard the grinding, sickening slash,
Of gleaming steel in the early light.

It was a charge that would not stop,
As we died in a furious flood.
And living was a chaotic rush to flaming
And life only barbed wire, pain, and blood.

And the young men cried out
"Dear Jesus, will the dying never end?"

Ken Sauvage
Corporal, USMC, 2nd Bn 3rd Marines,
Vietnam, 1968-1969

Jerking in Gepetto's hands
steel cables
controlling
weaving a web
a maze of paths and intersections

whirling at
the whim of the puppeteer
epileptic dances
across the stars.

Inside the wood is sound
but my mind is caught
in the web
and splintered strands
scrape memories.

Casualty of War

Sgt. Richard G. Lawrence
Combat Vietnam Veteran, USMC

"This is the way I see war. I still have all these things in my head and there is not a day I don't think about it."

12th Evac

Dana S.
1st Lieutenant, USA Nurse Corps, Vietnam

The hands remember what the mind evades:
death's quiet chill creeping from toes toward heart
the crepitation of pneumothorax
skin become pebbly where blasted with shrapnel
the tentative fluttering of terminal shock

The nightmares remember what the hands forget:
blowflies feasting on clotted bandages

the pounding of Hueys counting cadence for pulses
boots sliding and sticking in gore on the floor
the stormy tint of blasted bone
ranks of IV bottles clinking in chorus—
temple bells of mindfulness standing as sentinels
vigilant against the next crimson monsoon

The soul remembers what the heart disavows:
being mortally wounded by each soldier who died.

Door Gunner's Dream

Samuel D.
Sergeant, USMC, HMM-362 "Ugly Angels,"
Vietnam, 1968–1969

Rotors thumping, engines screaming,
My machine gun dealing out death.
I feel so alive, yet I'm so aware,
I may be taking my last breath.
Fire from below, my fire raining down,
My conscience screaming inside my mind.
Yet, my will to live, not wanting to die,
Lets me leave all my teachings behind.
Then, as I look down upon the carnage,
I can't believe what I've just seen.
And it's then that I awake and realize,
It's just another of my "door gunner's dreams."

Crucifixion Nam

Ralph "Tripper" Sirianni
Sergeant, USMC, 2nd Bn 7th Reg, Vietnam, 1969-1970

"Tet, 1969: The base was overrun. By the time we arrived,
there were bodies everywhere."

Earl Z.
Sergeant, USMC, Vietnam

I was discharged in 1969; for years after, I had nightmares, flashbacks, and an isolated attitude. I drank myself into a stupor every night so I could sleep. My marriage was in deep trouble, I lost job after job, and suicide was a serious option.

Since Vietnam, I've seen the world in a much different light. There is no camaraderie, people are all for one, and one for themselves. There seems to be no respect, no real team effort, no watching each other's back. I truly miss that.

0300 Da Nang 1972

Joyce C. "Flash" Olson Massello
Captain, USAFNCR, Flight Nurse 9th AEG,
Vietnam, 1972–1973

Sunrise . . .
Perpetual and new . . .
Our wounded patients look through
Plane windows with misted eyes
Freedom bird to Clark
Via a litter and flight crew
We've brought them out of war
Out of the horrors they knew
Rushing on an aircraft
Whose floor bounces with turbulence.
We try to still the fear, ease the pain
Help these men hold on to life again
Rocket, flares, storms, and SAMs
Are pointed our way
We joke, we close the C-9 shades
We don't think of fear—we only pray
To get our guys safely out of there
Later the fear comes—later the dreams
Of fiery crashes or wrong decisions
Men's hands we hold to calm the tremors
Our tremors are inside unseen
Lightning dances off the wings
A Marine sits up startled
We put on taped music for the soul
Rock and roll for the escape it brings
A man cries out in pain
Morphine eases his torment
We try to soothe his friends
Who love and worry at that moment
Would their friend join God without them?
Landing at the burn center we deplane
Our tortured air crewmen
They're drenched by monsoon rains
And we wonder will family hold them again

Who will hold me when their faces return
In my dreams to ask "Why us?"

The Loss of Innocence and Love

Charles Edward Elliott
Lance Corporal, USMC,
Dong Ha, Vietnam, 1967–1968

Sometimes we can still hear the screams
In our nightmares, our dreams
When does it all come to an end?

When we find our innocence and love again.

Robert Aldrich
Sergeant, USA, 2/39th Inf 9th Div,
Vietnam, 1968–1969

The war—it won't leave me
It creeps in at night
And shatters my brain
I must be insane.

Every Night After Johnny Carson

Kellan Kyllo
USMC, HMM-162, Ky Ha, Marble Mountain,
Quang Tri, Vietnam, 1966–1968

He kneeled behind the bed with his rifle,
didn't make a sound,
while

NVA troops walked into the house,
searched through each room,
and
then left.

———

Jerry T.
E-4, USA, 4th Inf Div, Vietnam

While walking down the street on a very hot day,
   I heard a truck backfire and my mind
      went far away

For a few minutes I was twenty years in
   my past

Hearing gunfire, men screaming, and rockets'
   blast

I heard the cry of ambush, I saw the
   point man fall

I said a quick prayer, "Please God, save us all."

As I was low crawling on the corner believing
   I was back in Nam.

People were looking and laughing at me, as if
   I was crazy or dumb

When the chopper came to pick up the bodies,
   the flashback fades away

But I'm still wondering why it couldn't have
   been me instead of the point man, who got
      Killed In Action that day!

Loss of Innocence—Arriving in Vietnam

Thomas N. "Tommy" Bills
Sergeant, USA, 2/7th Cav (Gary Owen Bde) 1st Cav Div

"My artwork is my healing, my opportunity to be the real me, to let others know that we can heal from the horrors of our past."

Flashbacks

Frank-Josip Racic
Sergeant, USA, Vietnam, 1968–1970

Reaching over grabbing the dark brown plastic handled
coffee pot that sat too close to a glowing red electric
burner left melted plastic in the palm of his hand
before he could set it back down.
Later that morning he recalled another time and another
place where it was hot, very hot.
It had been hot for days. One hundred and five in the
shade. Touching the barrel of his weapon burned his

fingers and it hadn't been fired all day.

The cold sweat soaked into the band of his helmet liner triggering flashbacks of when he was 10 and playing soldier in the flower-scented rain. Now the smell of death hung heavy in the night air as the sounds of corpses popping continued to ring through his ears long after he saw how the hot sun decomposed a pile of corpses hideously stacked in Auschwitz style along the road where earlier that morning all hell broke loose in what seemed to be an endless firefight.

There Is a *Fear*

Michael Rice
RM-2, USN, PBR River Boats,
Dong Ha River Security Group,
Cua Viet River, Vietnam, 1968-1969

Somewhere in my mind lies a point between my conscious and sub-conscious.

I can dream it, remember it, anticipate it, and try to plan for it. And whether I am awake, or asleep, out from the depths, like a crazed demon, it comes. Unmercifully, all enveloping and soul possessing it comes, it comes, it so damn surely comes.

You are flung back as if it were happening right then. The smell, the flashes, the concussions, the explosions, the smell, the smell, the God awful smell of powder and flesh and blood and screaming and crying and swearing . . .

"Those God damn Bastard Sons of Bitches" . . .

The smell, the smell. The helplessness of being only one against eternity. You scream out in desperation. No one can hear. Nor could you hear if anyone cried out for help and comfort in his last conscious instant. Another flash and concussion and a scream silenced too soon. You know another is gone forever.

No, not forever God, please not forever.

And then it is over. No one has seen you vulnerable. You are *safe*, then, now, and yesterday's tomorrow. In your dream-past you are *alive* and can even smile. In your conscious-present no one has sensed that you were back *there*. They will not think you insane or crazy. You have won another battle. But . . .

Out of the black, your Future self stares. It is your inner psyche, your soul, your utter existence. There is a *fear* there. A fear that only those who have stepped to the edge and looked into oblivion know. Only they and those who have stepped over forever know it. A fear that I wish upon no one.

I hope for the sake of the 58,000 KIA and the veterans who have killed themselves since the Vietnam conflict that the nightmares do end with this life and the other side is all loving and peaceful. Maybe they can hear and see us and wish they could comfort us and tell us not to cry. Because there, there is no more fear.

Experience of Transference

Edward J. Burris
Vietnam

This is not then
This is now
This is not that
This is this.
Then why?
Why?
Does it feel like this
Does it feel like then?

After Nam

Alan B.
E-5, Vietnam, 1969–1970

Thoughts of war are in my head, all the time I see the dead.

The pain, the agony, and the suffering we were prepared for, but not in life, only in war.

Agent Orange, the DVA, POW/MIA, is this the government's way of helping, or the way that it betrays?

PTSD what's that mean? Put in a claim and you'll see.

What does it mean to be a vet? Mistrust in mankind is my bet.

Faithfully serve the red, white, and blue, is this what you'll tell your son to do?

———

Ken Sauvage
Corporal, USMC, 2nd Bn 3rd Marines,
Vietnam, 1968–1969

The explosion of bullets
shatters a prison womb
of narrowly constructed years
and I live,
but once having kissed death;
love's first crush
in the spring of adolescence,
her image remains
etched on my eyes
and all that I see
shimmers
in the power of her presence.

———

Clyde Q.
Corporal, USMC (R),
South Korea, 1950–1951

As a confederate soldier said during the American Civil War, "It's a rich man's war and a poor man's fight."

Poppy Day

Ken Sauvage
Corporal, USMC, 2nd Bn 3rd Marines,
Vietnam, 1968–1969

Red poppies drip from wounds
long since scarred over
flowing past rows and rows of beds—
steel and starch—
and down disinfected corridors
into the streets.

NUMBING

Vets do not submissively accept falling victim to their past. They will
do all in their power to resist the flood of memories, feelings, and
nightmares that bend them to whatever has hurt or terrified them. Frequently, veterans will attempt to escape from memories entirely, hiding
whole portions of their combat tour from themselves.

When forgetfulness isn't sufficient to ward off the pain, vets may
resort to other, more desperate measures, such as alcohol and drugs, to
gain dreamless sleep and erase the caring. They may distance themselves from their world and those people and things that serve as reminders, or tempt them to relinquish a tight hold on their feelings. But
these measures are never enough, and often alienate those around the
veteran, leaving him or her alone with their memories.

Rosemary A.
USA, Vietnam

After my return to the United States I had a major burial . . . my memory. I put everything away so far I never thought it would surface, and
it worked, or so I thought for the better part of 23 years, through two
unsuccessful marriages. I became an RN and could function well only

in a trauma-ER setting . . . there I was tops and continue 19 years later. Then all of a sudden I had terrible nightmares, awoke drenched in my own sweat, could see faces I hadn't remembered for years, certain sounds such as thunder bothered me terribly. I was becoming nothing but a raw nerve and was so wired with my thoughts that I wanted to simply end it all, just to have some peace.

A Combat Scenario

James F. Sedgley
Platoon Sergeant, USA, 1st Plt, Co E,
184th Inf Reg 7th Inf Div
W.W. II: Aleutian Islands, Kwajalein, Philippines, Okinawa

Okinawa in the Ryukyus, home ground of the enemy—April 1, 1945—the island looked peaceful, no resistance on the beachhead. We were lucky; we went ashore. The less fortunate sailors, with their landing craft, had to return to their mother ships and weather the storm that Kamikaze planes rained down for hours as we watched from shore. War? Why! Coordinated manslaughter? Or, could it be sanctioned murder?

Our progress went unchecked for a few days. We had turned south, and then encountered sporadic sniping. We continued to move forward.

Then, all H—— broke loose—all the weapons of modern warfare seemed to be in use, even the Navy's big guns were firing, their flares turning night into day. Fortunately or unfortunately, during front-line combat, neither side goes home at night. Yes, we even fought on weekends and holidays.

Such a cacophony of sound while those instruments of death took their toll: Ours on them and theirs on us. Bullets, mortar fragments, artillery shells all are lethal. The proof was everywhere, even across my back. Worse yet, when I was hit by those mortar fragments, two of my men (just behind me) were killed by fragments from the same shell.

Then, the accumulated effects of sustained exposure to that which man was not meant to endure, surfaced: one of my men jumped up screaming, turned to the rear, threw down his rifle, and ran headlong to

- - - - - ? (I wonder if he could ever stop running from this assault on his mind?) He had always been a good soldier!

The number of days is vague. I know for the most part that each minute consumed days and each hour was an eternity.

The mind leaves the scene, the views are detached. You ask permission to go for a new dressing on your hand, some treatment for your back, and for a brief respite from the "horror." You arrive at the forward aid station. Then, next morning you're aboard a hospital ship and it is traveling east.

Epilogue. Thank God I survived, I think!

Honorably discharged, Oct. 4, 1945, Certificate of Disability.

Caught a bus from the Convalescent Hospital at Camp Atterbury, Indiana and got home in a couple of days. Got off the bus in Auburn, just across the street from the train station, where Mom saw us off, over four years before. I called home and quietly waited until my younger sister drove in from the farm. When we got home, I changed into Levi's.

Author's note: These recollections are dedicated to those men of
Company E, 184th Infantry Regiment, my Comrades-in-Arms,
during those four years of war, Heroes all (less one)!

Amnesia

Kellan Kyllo
USMC, HMM-162, Ky Ha, Marble Mountain,
Quang Tri, Vietnam, 1966–1968

Everything that had ever happened to him
in Vietnam
was recorded,
but hidden somewhere.

Clyde Q.
Corporal, USMC (R), South Korea, 1950–1951

For so many years I shut the memories of Korea out of my mind. I carried on my life as normally as possible and acted as though nothing had ever happened. But now the memories have surfaced.

It is difficult to suppress my emotions, especially when I see a military funeral, or a movie depicting a young soldier or Marine's life gradually slipping away as he whispers to his buddy to tell his parents or wife how he died.

Dead Hero

Charles Felix
Corporal, USMC, W.W. II:
Bougainville, Guam, Iwo Jima

They brought him back at noontime
At noon as chow was served.
Down the muddy track of Piva
A blood smeared half-track for his hearse.

It carried him down to the beach
Amid the wreckage at Torokina.
To lie in maggot strewn dignity
Awaiting the grave detail.

This was a warrior's end
And dead white feet with rigid toes widespread.
Seemed to wave an uncertain farewell
As his armored hearse jolted away.

And we turned back to chow.

For it was not us who had died,
That day.

Author's note: Dedicated to Donald Johnson, killed on Bougainville and awarded the Navy Cross. It seemed cruel for him to die.

Crawling Around Indian Country

Dennis R. Tenety
Lance Corporal, USMC (Ret), 1st Marine Division
India Co 1st Plt 3rd Bn 5th Reg, An Hoa, Vietnam, 1969

What does it mean when you hear your pulse beating through your ears? When I sleep, why do I come right out of it; not knowing where I am, crawling around for what feels like hours?

If it ain't Nam, it's revenge. I realize I made a promise that day and now the time is closing as the "minutes get madder."

I lose days. I don't remember everything. My head is always in Nam.

I realize now that there were about eight salts in India Co.; me being the FNG. The rest made about 30 days. There was never time to place their names with their faces. The ops ran. Continuous months spent in the bush with ground pounding. In my eight months, I only remember one show, one visit to the E club; that was when we lost too many to friendly fire, humped back to the rear, stayed a day, then humped our asses into what was called Indian Country, "Arizona." All the time thinking of when I get back to "the world."

Shit man, you hated a place called Nam only to find all along you loved it.

Daniel D.
USA, First Lieutenant, 2Bn 7th Cav 1st Cav Div, Vietnam, 1967–1969

The combat soldier in Vietnam lived in a world of
Constant fear, punctuated by brief episodes of
Terror or rage. Even among brothers-in-arms, only
The fear could be talked about, and then only seldom.
Openly acknowledging the terror or rage was not
Done—the risk was losing control, the price was your
Sanity. And, because your brothers were like you
In this regard, the terror and rage were never
Acknowledged. For many veterans today, they are still
Difficult to acknowledge.

Vietnam Remembered

John Malick
E-5, USA, 101st Airborne TDY
197th Trans., Vietnam, 1970–1972

I sat alone
my back pressed against
cold concrete,
as the human race passed,
I struggled to sit upright . . .

At the end of my bottle,
as easy as the last drink
it became clear . . .

My wife gone,
the kids at their Aunt's,
me
out in the cold . . .

Vietnam sucked . . .

Robert di G.
Private First Class, USA, Vietnam, 1969

PTSD was a condition that existed in Nam, only there wasn't any "post" about it. It compounded itself, depending upon the amount of horror and pain you experienced; it was always present and is difficult to write about. It involved the NVA, the VC, the heat, the impenetrable jungle, the monsoon season, the diseases, the culture, the violence, the fear, the drugs.

It has been called America's only teenage war. I was 18 in Nam as were most of my compadres. I read that 85 percent of those killed were teenagers. When I returned from Nam I couldn't vote or legally buy liquor. As the song by Barry McGuire said, "Old enough to kill, but not for voting!" I was deceived by the status quo, the government, the military, and my own emotions.

I am 42-years-old now and have never held a job for more than a year. I've had more than 40 different jobs, I lived in 21 states, 49 cities, and three foreign countries since 1969. I have been divorced twice, lost my children in the second one. The courts decided I was unstable, had PTSD, and awarded the mother full custody. She was allowed to leave Washington state, where we resided, and move to Alaska. I have only seen my children for a few hours during the last year. They are four and six. I call weekly, but lately the children don't want to talk to me.

Hidden Victims

Margaret Cole Marshall, Lt. Col., USAF, NC (Ret)
Cyndi Krampitz Linkes, Capt., USAF, NC (Ret)
Operation Desert Storm

Military nurses take care of patients who have been physically traumatized by war and in the process nurses become subject to the same horrors. People think because nurses are not on front lines they cannot suffer from post-traumatic stress disorder. Seeing and hearing things beyond human comprehension, they have difficulty making sense of the atrocities.

Nurses see themselves as professionals who give care. They are used to helping others. The problem is they do not acknowledge that they themselves can become emotional casualties of war. Seeing people terribly injured or disfigured by war affects them greatly. Nurses have to make quick decisions regarding peoples' lives, decisions with which they must live forever. It isn't easy.

Reserve unit nurses returned from Desert Storm one or two at a time. One nurse got off the aircraft, quit her civilian job, and disappeared. She came back to the United States frustrated and disillusioned by what she experienced. Others came back changed, some depressed, others upset and angry, others sad. Marital problems, interpersonal problems, job and financial problems were all symptoms.

Initially, nursing staff were reluctant to share feelings and trust others in their unit. There was anger, fear, and concern. There were organizational and leadership problems, difficulties with co-workers and poor communication with family members. Relationships were falling apart due to stress. Staff were concerned with re-establishing previous civilian lifestyles. Jobs they once had were no longer there. Outlooks or philosophies of life changed due to the deployment. It was a very difficult time which nurses needed to work through as part of the transition home. They needed support from the organization and each other. They needed to understand they are human, too, and have the same emotional needs as their patients. They needed nurturing and support so the next time they are deployed, they can meet the challenges and better adapt to stress. Without this, their experiences lead to a full blown combat stress reaction that can affect them negatively for life.

He Never Let Anyone Hurt Him Again

Kellan Kyllo
USMC, HMM-162, Ky Ha, Marble Mountain,
Quang Tri, Vietnam, 1966–1968

Whenever he was around people
he watched carefully,
looked into their eyes,
read
their faces,
each and every one of them
as they passed.

Walking Alone

Adrian S.
USMC, Vietnam

When the world is full of people, but you can't live with yourself; coping is a difficult task because you feel like walking alone.

When the everyday problems surround you and reality hits you smack in the face that the world doesn't give a damn about you, that's when you feel like walking alone.

When I let my problems overwhelm me and the little things seem so big, that's when I feel like walking alone.

When it seems it takes forever to return home from Vietnam twenty-five years ago, that's when I feel like I'm walking alone.

When the lovers that I had are no longer there, when my friends have all died or been taken away, that's when I feel like I'm walking alone.

When I am just sitting and thinking about things gone bad and not thinking about the good, that's when I feel like I'm walking alone.

When I feel I have lost all need to go on, but know in my heart that it just can't be true, why in the hell do I feel like I'm walking all alone?

Author's note: From a Vietnam vet with PTSD to my brothers:
There is help. We do not have to walk alone.

Branded a Loser

Charles Edward Elliott
Lance Corporal, USMC,
Dong Ha, Vietnam, 1967–1968

It was hard for me to understand
After fighting for this land
In a country called Vietnam,
I was now a branded man,
Hated by the country I had served.
It was something I did not deserve.
It made me stop and wonder why
All my brothers had to die,
Many by my side.
Many times I wanted to cry
But I kept it deep inside.
The things people in this country would say
Would slowly eat me away.
Something they could never see
Was all the hurt and pain, deep inside of me.

I wanted so very much to come back home
And leave the fighting zone.
Instead, I ended up all alone
Without a country, without a home,
Branded a loser.

2

ISOLATION

"But deep down inside, all the mothers knew,
America had quit on him."
Gregory Schlieve

Many early cultures required a ritual purification of the soldier returned from war. Some were housed separately, in "warrior's houses," until such purification could occur. After the warrior was purified, he re-entered the community of his fellows. All of this means that the warrior, as well as his friends, family, and community recognized and accepted the reality of the warrior's participation in combat, accepted the fact that he was changed by it, and that he needed to be re-integrated and welcomed into society upon his return.

The undeclared wars of this century did not permit this "orderly" flow of acknowledgment, support, and purification. The police action in Korea and the conflict in Vietnam were not acknowledged as "real" wars, by those other than the participants. If veterans are not acknowledged, they are rejected, then ignored, then left in bitter isolation.

Vets write in anger at being reviled or ignored by their country and their countrymen as well as the people they fought to save. They are bitter at being denied the modern-day equivalent of the warrior's purification rite—their homecoming parade. Vets have long memories and carry their bitterness for many years, while society expects them to forget the past and move on to other things. Society pays little heed as vets continue to demand the "purification" and acceptance they never received. Rejection is a vicious circle, and the danger for returned warriors is that they continue to isolate themselves and reject those around them long after society has put the war behind it, and has lost the capacity to accept the vet on his exacting terms. Unless vets move *themselves* towards acceptance, their sense of isolation will persist forever.

A Soldier Returns Home

Gregory Schlieve
Sergeant, USA, Co C 5/7
1st Air Cav Div, Vietnam, 1969

He came home all numbed up,
Had done some killing, but wasn't proud of it.
Was just happy to be home,
But in his mind, he couldn't believe he'd made it.

Now, all he wanted was to be . . .
To be the person he was . . . before he went away.
But the thoughts kept returning,
Couldn't stop the thoughts of killing, try hard as he may.

W.W. II vets did not understand him,
What's happened to this vet? He seems to have gone crazy.
Said he wasn't like the vets before,
Said he was full of rage, and that he was lazy.

But the question kept returning,
What's with this vet? He's so different from the others.
No one dared to speak,
It was much too shameful, let's not tell his mother.

And no one said a word,
America chose to numb itself, the deed was much too grim.
But deep down inside,
All the mothers knew, America had quit on him.

Clyde Q.
Corporal, USMC (R), South Korea, 1950–1951

I feel depressed, and at times angry.

Angry at the President who sent us there in the first place . . . and
angry because he then called our mission "only a police action." Angry
at the unappreciative people that we were fighting to save.

Dennis R. Tenety
Lance Corporal, USMC (Ret), 1st Marine Division
India Co 1st Plt 3rd Bn 5th Reg, An Hoa, Vietnam, 1969

Your answer to tame me was to chain my wings, put me under your thumb. Never will it happen! I despise you, for it was you who sent me into battle. I know the price of freedom. Your money can't buy back my losses. I have my spirit. It grows stronger every time you try to take more from me. In the end it is I who will win.

Ralph "Tripper" Sirianni
Sergeant, USMC, 2nd Bn 7th Reg,
Vietnam, 1969–1970

Bitterness can be a handicap. You go through life with a deep-rooted resentment that spreads like cancer. All those who are close to you are affected.

Nam can't be compared to anything. We were stabbed in the back and had to learn to live with it. The mayor of our fine city, before a crowd of hundreds (maybe thousands), referred to Nam vets as "belly-achers." This was the same guy that came around praising us at election time. We didn't all dig a hole and stay in it. The Vietnam vet kicked up a lot of dust to get the benefits all veterans receive today.

The Combat Vet

Written at VAMC Marion, Indiana on December 4, 1988
Paul W. Scalf
Lance Corporal, USMC, Battery F, 2nd Bn 11th Marine Reg
1st MarDiv, I Corps Vietnam, 1968–1969

The combat vet is a man who came home
to live free, and love, but still is alone.
He lives in a mind filled with anger and pain

and walks through a world of darkness and rain.
He lives in a world where society's rules
view his medals for valor as priceless jewels
yet treats their wearer as if he was dirt
and rewards him with insults, scorn, and hurt.

The combat vet had scored many kills
for his country, but now they treat him with pills.
"Take this pill and that pill
And soon you will see;
You'll be cured and be normal again,
Just like me!"
But our PTSD can't be cured just like that
nor are we helped by burning our hats.
Treating PTSD takes many years of time
and patience and love to soothe our minds.

The combat vet has a right to his anger.
He was sent to a land filled with death and danger.
His country betrayed him yet told him he should
never let it affect him . . . to always be good
like the well-trained soldier he's supposed to be
and die without questioning his country.

The combat vet risked his life, soul, and heart
to fight in a war which still tears him apart.
His country now tells him, "Be proud of your deeds!"
while looking at him like a lawn full of weeds.
They drenched him with a deadly aerial spray
and told him it would keep the mosquitoes away.
His body is dying, his children deformed
yet the government refuses to keep him informed.
They deny Agent Orange and keep telling lies
while every day more of these combat vets die
of horrible cancers and all types of ills
and all they do is give us more pills.

The government will not open society's gate
and welcome us home until it's too late.
"They'll never fit in here," the government said,

"until every one of them, finally, is dead."
But when that day happens, our spirits will know
that we finally won that war fought so long ago.

Home Front

Dennis R. Tenety
Lance Corporal, USMC (Ret), 1st Marine Division
India Co 1st Plt 3rd Bn 5th Reg, An Hoa, Vietnam, 1969

You shunned us on our return. You spit on us. You labeled us Baby Killers, crazed Vietnam vets. There were no parades. We were the first to lose a war. You gave no honor to our dead. Families and friends mourned alone. Why not? It was appropriate, alone we departed, alone we returned.

Our country called. The brave answered. The cowards ran. The war raged on. The likes of Fonda and the educated of Berkeley abetted the enemy and the enemy fought on the morale you fed them. Some of our own came home only to turn against our cause. Yes, they called *you* the brave, you who protested for your beliefs.

Fifteen years later your guilt beat you. You gave us a parade. (You also got your amnesty.) Finally America honored her dead; admitted they were ours. The guilt, you thought, was purged from your bowels. "We're sorry." "Welcome home!" The Domino Theory proved true. Ask the Cambodians, then ask the Laotians. Then ask yourself, "How many of the over 58,000 did I help the enemy slay in battle?"

Yet you only ask why so many of us are still bitter. Sleep my dreams for one night, live my experiences for one day, then ask me why I am the way I am.

Clyde Q.
Corporal, USMC (R), South Korea, 1950–1951

As a 19-year-old Marine with 11 months of continuous combat, a Chinese Army artillery shell exploded within a few feet of my foxhole. The concussion knocked me out. When I awoke, I was being taken to the med-evac station.

At the Army hospital in Taegu, South Korea, the bespectacled Army psychiatrist sat before me asking me stupid questions. His demeanor and choice of words gave me the feeling that he thought I was shirking my duty as a Marine. He wrote things down as I cursed President Harry Truman, the Chinese, South Korea, and the whole damn political structure. After three weeks in the hospital I was released back to duty, but was not considered fit for combat.

Cross and Star

Tracey D. W. M.
USA, Vietnam

Paranoid and alone
men stand surrounded
by smashed out windows
from drunken nights
and broken lives.

Soft treading soldiers
not wanting to warn
circle with hate-filled
eyes as they lock
the door and throw
away the key.

Hide your Frankensteins.
A government hoped
to gain much but
the war is over
and many warriors came home.

That same government
denies responsibility
while shifting blame,
like sand upon the shore,
it's focused on the men
who fought and died
in Vietnam.

The Pawns of Vietnam

Robert Aldrich
Sergeant, USA, 2/39th, Inf 9th Div,
Vietnam, 1968–1969

Does anybody care about us,
Does anybody care?
Does anybody care about us,
If so, we know not where.

You sent us off to our despair,
With little time for us to prepare.
You sent us off to our demise,
With so little time to realize.

You sent us to kill them, and them us.
So what the hell is all the fuss?
It's drug and drink in steady streams,
As we try to ease these awful dreams!

We seek retreat in solitude,
To find escape from your attitudes.
Our senseless deaths by our own hands,
But still, you don't try to understand.

Bad memories branded into our brains,
You're affecting our children with your disdain.
You left us hanging out to dry,
To find our way, ourselves we try.

Who should really feel the shame,
From protest, accusation, and wrongful blame?
"Not us!" I say, we were but tools,
Used with waste by political fools.

We fought, we lived, we died inside,
And we came home, but no one cried.
Will we ever fight the same?
Not on your life—we're not insane!

Fifty jobs within ten years,
Gallons and gallons of frustrated tears.
Used, abused, and torn with grief,
But no one offers needed relief.

Our only way seems life in seclusion,
Do you find it sad to reach this conclusion?
No, we don't expect you to understand,
We know we're pawns, no longer in demand!

Does anybody care about us,
Does anybody care?
Does anybody care about us,
If so, we know not where.

———————

Duane A. "Tubby" Brudvig
Specialist/5, USA, Vietnam, 1969-1970

I wish I knew that I was going to have all these feelings later on after
the war, like my uncles did after W.W. II. They suffered. They drank.
They cried. They hurt. All this stuff should have been explained; there
should have been help available at the VA. Instead it let us down. It was
a breach of contract! We joined and served with the understanding that
our government would care for us after the war. Well, where was it?

Coming Back to the World

Jerry T.
E-4, USA, 4th Inf Div, Vietnam

I left Nam with so much honor and pride,
After the plane landed all my hopes and dreams died.
"Hey America!!!" you crush me very well,
I'm just a man in an empty shell.
Can't hold my head up, no not yet,
I'm still ashamed of being a Vietnam vet.
One day I hope that I can say, "A Vietnam vet I'm proud to be,"
That's once I find the real me.

Dana S.
1st Lieutenant, USA Nurse Corps, Vietnam

Being a woman with PTSD is a real double bind. My need for under-standing and empathy always seems to run straight up against society's expectations about what I, as a woman, am supposed to be doing with my life, namely, taking care of everyone else.

If, when I am feeling particularly depressed, vulnerable, and ex-hausted, I attempt to get my husband to make his own dinner and give me some time to myself, he sulks like a puppy. Most of the time it's easier to ignore my own feelings and needs and attend to my husband's rather than to do battle to gain a reprieve from my routine household duties. He can be quite sympathetic—as long as my problem doesn't inconvenience him too much. But if my emotional state ruins his evening out or disrupts his plans for me to take care of something for him, I am faced with the enervating task of simultaneously dealing with my emotional problem and his exasperation. If my leg was bro-ken, he would manage to fend for himself. My heart is broken, yet I am expected to be unobtrusive about it, lest I place any untoward demands on him.

PTSD is not the psychological equivalent of a cold. It's more like lupus—it's chronic, unpredictable, multi-symptomed, and dangerous as hell. My female upbringing instilled, and my training as a nurse reinforced, the notion that if I can't take care of everyone else's needs, I have no value; I have failed in my primary role; I am not moral. So I take care of everyone else's needs and feel angry and resentful that they don't take care of mine, even when I make a direct, clear request. Part of the problem is that my husband—along with most other people—doesn't take emotional problems seriously unless those problems are totally incapacitating. I function professionally at a very high level while being seriously overdrawn emotionally. This is my way of trying to fend off PTSD. At work no one ever knows I spent the night awake crying, or in nightmare after nightmare. My husband also embraces the comforting but erroneous assumption that so long as I appear to be "normal" most of the time, then my condition can't be very serious. After all, I'm not one of those unemployed, homeless, unkempt vets whose illness is instantly visible and therefore he doesn't have to exert any extra effort or alter his comfort level on my behalf. I feel devalued, discounted, deprecated. I'm not loved "for free"—only for what I can do within my role as a wife/caretaker. I think I should be getting more value for the emotional price I paid. But no one seems to place much value on caring. It's just another part of "women's work"—underpaid, underrated, and taken for granted until it's no longer provided.

I get tired of being the scapegoat for every problem in my marriage and family relationships because of my PTSD. It seems to me that the person in the relationship with the formal diagnosis is conveniently assumed to be the source of all the problems in that relationship. Having PTSD doesn't automatically invalidate my point of view, negate my perceptions, or make me the one who needs to change my behavior. Although I have an emotional problem, I'm neither retarded nor psychotic. I don't use a psychiatric diagnosis as an excuse not to get up and go to work or to avoid family responsibilities; likewise, my family shouldn't use my diagnosis as a cop-out for their irresponsibility towards me.

America the Beautiful

Kellan Kyllo
USMC, HMM-162, Ky Ha, Marble Mountain,
Quang Tri, Vietnam, 1966-1968

O beautiful.
Old friends ridiculed them for Vietnam.
For spacious skies.
Strangers condemned them, too.
For amber waves of grain.
Nightmares and flashbacks.
For purple mountains majesty.
Trembling lives.
Above the fruited plain.
America,
America,
God shed His grace on thee.
Only those who were there with them, only they know.
And crown thy good.
Now they're all living and hiding secretly.
With brotherhood.
Waiting.
From sea.
For the war to finally end inside them.
To shining sea.
With peace.

Editors' note: "America" was frequently sung by U.S. troops
at the end of USO shows in Vietnam.

Anonymous
Captain, French Army, Upon His Return from Dien Bien Phu
(Courtesy of Gregory Schlieve)

We turned in upon ourselves,
we lived among ourselves, and we became touchy

and sensitive as men flayed.
But how great was the despair
we felt at being rejected by our country
and how great was our need of fraternity.

Editors' note: All that is known about this poem is that it was posted on a
bulletin board at American Lake VA Hospital in Tacoma, WA.

John J. Lennox
Staff Sergeant, USA, "A" Btry 10th Field Artillery Bn
3rd Inf Div, Korea, 1950–51
Sergeant First Class, USA, 1099th Medium Boat Co Mobile Riverine Force,
Cat Lai, Mekong Delta, Vietnam, 1968-1969

"Don't mean nuthin don't work anymore."

It's said that when you become older, you become more forgetful. I may forget where I put my glasses, car keys, or wallet, but some things I'll never forget—like being scared, homesick, lonely, dirty, forgotten, betrayed, cold, and wet. I remember being in a foxhole in Korea when it was 15 below. I will always remember the heat of Vietnam—God, it was like a blast furnace coming at you from all directions.

Being forgetful is not a big deal, but trying to forget the unforgettable is to deny that it ever happened. That will screw up your head so bad, that if you don't seek help, it will never unscrew. PTSD is treatable, there is hope. We are not crazy. You have got to talk about what happened in the war. Your enemy now is your memory.

There's a tape in our heads, and when the play button is pushed, you once again see the dead and the dying. You see your buddy with a hole in his chest and smell the burning villages. "Don't mean nuthin" will not make the images go away. Everything you saw and did on your tour has to be talked about with someone who understands. You don't need medication—you need understanding. Help is there, so for God's sake do it now!

Editors' note: "Don't mean nuthin" was a common phrase uttered and written
on helmets by emotionally exhausted front-line veterans in Vietnam.

3

SEEKING HELP

"Finding appropriate therapy for PTSD can be as much a trauma as
PTSD itself, especially for women vets. The female director of one
Vet Center . . . chirped about what male vets were like . . . just what I
needed: a therapist who sounded like Tweety Bird in heat."
Dana S.

"We survived the fight. Special thanks to all the people at the
Vet Center. Thank God for your helping hand."
Charles Edward Elliott

Asking for help is a difficult task for veterans who prided themselves in
saving their buddies' lives in action, or the lives and limbs of the
wounded. It's as if asking for help is an admission of weakness. This is
strange, if you think of it. Who thought their comrade weak for crying,
"CORPSMAN!"? Which nurse or doctor thought the less of a soldier,
sailor, or Marine for his moans or whimpers in the Evac?

Seeking help for combat trauma is not like going to the emergency room to bandage a wound. A bleeding patient understands a

wound, and although afraid, knows that the bleeding can be stanched and the wound healed. In a very deep wound, the patient may fear loss of function, a fear that can usually be quickly confirmed or put to rest by the physician. In either case, the patient has a good idea of what to expect. A veteran with PTSD has no similar frame of reference. He and she lack not only an understanding of the nature of a psychological wound, but initially deny its existence. When a vet begins to suspect that there is a wound, and that it is combat-related, the impulse to deny it can grow even stronger. Driven by feelings of crumbling pride and mounting fear that are confusing and painful to express, the decision to seek help is often an act of desperation for a man or woman who has long suffered in isolation.

In many parts of the country, obtaining treatment for combat-related trauma, certainly obtaining free care, means going to "the V.A." The decision to seek help from a federal agency poses a significant hurdle for veterans who condemn governmental bodies as the cause of their problems. After rejecting and feeling rejected by society, vets are forced not only to admit their "weakness" to a stranger, but also to invest something they have jealously guarded for many years—their trust.

Despair. Mistrust. Fear. It requires a great deal of courage to walk into a V.A. Hospital or a Veterans Outreach Center for the first time. It requires greater courage to stay. The pain in memories revealed through therapy is an unexpected shock to many veterans and they may begin to question their decision to seek help. Sometimes, the pain taxes therapists' ability to help veterans cope with the memories revealed by a therapist's probing.

Veterans' writings are highly polarized about their willingness to seek help and the quality of the help they receive, and reflect their confidence as well as their mistrust in caregivers.

Many write positively of the help they receive through the Outreach programs. "You can lead a productive life with PTSD . . . but you have to stay with the Vet Center program . . . ." writes one Marine. For some, group therapy provides the strong sense of belonging, or of family, that the veteran feels has been lost. Others express extreme frustration over years of fighting "the system." Making many unsuccessful attempts to get help increases veterans' skepticism and distrust. Women face the additional obstacle of being ignored as veterans, or having their service minimized by their fellow male vets, spouse, or both male and female treatment professionals. The key to many vets is finding a good counselor who will see them through the course of their therapy. This can take years, and is as much subject to the vagaries of federal funding as to the realities of a highly mobile work force.

Yet the intensity of their need compels veterans to keep reaching out for help from family and professionals, some of whom are ready and trained to respond, and some of whom are not. Those veterans who write of an imperfect system, who damn the V.A. and Outreach Centers, or the drugs with which they feel forced to maintain their lives, still do not write of "giving up." Their poems and essays have a sense of stubborn pride and determination, as if once the decision to obtain help is made, the goal of healing becomes obsessive. Some, disillusioned with federally-sponsored counseling, even use their own resources to obtain help in the private sector. And help is a two-way street. Counselors, both veteran and non-veteran, note the impact of the help they give both in the lives of their patients, and in their own.

"Seeking help" for combat trauma, can prove a complex undertaking, and can take many paths, but the paths have a common theme: not giving up.

Ken Sauvage
Corporal, USMC, 2nd Bn 3rd Marines,
Vietnam, 1968–1969

Before I started writing and drawing of my involvement in the Vietnam War, the feelings were roaming around inside of me, not recognized, and spilling out periodically in very non-productive and self-destructive ways. The strongest feelings were anger, guilt, and depression with a little high anxiety thrown in to make it interesting. When I got back from Vietnam, the first emotion to surface was a terrible anger. I was angry that the majority of the people in this country were unaware, seemingly by choice, of the horror that was taking place in their name. The only people who seemed to recognize the horror of the war were the anti-war groups.

I spent the first five years after Vietnam in complete denial. It was the anxiety attacks that pushed me to seek counseling. I realized I was in drastic need of doing some changing.

Randall L. Lusk
Staff Sergeant, USA Special Forces (Ret)

My name is Randall L. Lusk, SSGT, U.S. Army (Ret.). I served a total of 12 years on active duty. From August '78 to November '84 and October '85 to October '91. I served in the following conflicts: Central America ('80-'82), Lebanon ('83), Grenada ('83), Panama ('89-'90) and the Gulf ('90-'91). I served in the following units: C Co. 1/504 P.I.R. 82nd ABN Div, HHQ Marksmanship Training Unit 101st ABN Div, C Co. 1/75th Ranger Battalion, 5th 7th, 10th Special Forces Group, 1st Special Operations Command. And the 10th Special Forces Group attached to the USMC's 24 MAU in Beirut, Lebanon. My primary military occupational specialties were: Special Forces Light Weapons and Demolition Specialists, Combat Medic, Airborne Ranger Infantry, NBC Specialists, Military Policeman. I was medically retired on 10-4-91 at 100 percent service-connected disability and on Social Security after my 6th Purple Heart.

I've had my problems with PTSD. I've already been through four divorces. I tried alcohol for awhile, however the problems were always there when I sobered up. For the first several years on active duty I held onto all the noble beliefs of patriotism and ideas that drive most professional soldiers. However, when I started working for special operations things began to change.

I was medically retired after spending many years in military hospitals. But because so many of my operations were classified, it took me the next several years to get many of my medical records de-classified so that I could get the proper care that I needed. By this time I knew I had been deceived by the military, and bitterness set in with a vengeance. My physical condition got worse, and my distrust for the government mounted.

I had been brought up in a church believing that human life was sacred and now I was faced with the fact that I had done just the opposite, taken another human's life. The thought left me confused. I really don't know what God thought about me killing people, and I wasn't sure that He would ever forgive me for it. My life has become an array of shattered dreams. If I did all those things for "God and Country" then why was I being rejected like this?

It's still a daily battle we fight to control our emotions and deal with the world around us. Also, it's difficult for family members to understand the depths of emotions that run through us at times and why we react in a "combat mode" to certain situations. However, things do get somewhat easier with time, but it's a continual battle that we must fight.

Just remember—An American Never Gives Up!

Dana S.
1st Lieutenant, USA Nurse Corps, Vietnam

Finding appropriate therapy for PTSD can be as much a trauma as PTSD itself, especially for women vets. When the Vet Centers first opened, I went to one because I suspected that my recurrent depressions might have something to do with Vietnam, since they certainly couldn't be attributed to current circumstances. I was told that women don't get PTSD. The counselor I spoke to seemed to have about as much awareness of what nurses did in Vietnam as I did about growing pineapples in Alaska.

A few years later I developed symptoms that left no doubt in my mind that I had PTSD: I couldn't eat or sleep. I had nightmares about Vietnam. Household smells such as mildew or meat provoked flashbacks and reveries that lasted for hours. Constantly preoccupied with memories of Vietnam, I lost my concentration and organization at work. I didn't pay attention to TV shows, books, or conversations. I lost my temper over things that I normally wouldn't even notice. I became jumpy in crowds and dived into the dirt at sudden noises.

It was time to find help. Initially, I called upon the government that had sent me to Vietnam in the first place. Notwithstanding her professed delight that a woman veteran was calling, the female director of one Vet Center wasted a half hour of my time chirping about what male veterans were like. Just what I needed: a therapist who sounded like Tweety Bird in heat. I called another Vet Center; a recorded message told me that the entire staff was on a retreat for a week. "If you feel you have an emergency, please contact the nearest VA Hospital." If they could close the entire place down for a week, they must not be taking veterans' problems very seriously. So much for the system. I decided to pay my own way. I wanted a therapist who got his paycheck only if I was satisfied. It worked.

Ralph "Tripper" Sirianni
Sergeant, USMC, 2nd Bn 7th Reg,
Vietnam, 1969–1970

Being a federal employee, it was hard for me to be totally honest with the doctor diagnosing me. Just like the medals, some guys deserve them and others don't. That's the whole deal with PTSD and it's an injustice.

James F. Sedgley
Platoon Sergeant, USA, 1st Plt Co E 184th Inf Reg 7th Inf Div,
W.W. II: Aleutian Islands, Kwajalein, Philippines, Okinawa

Chronology of Medical Care by the VA

Okinawa—10 April 1945—an Aide Station—required treatment for shrapnel wounds on back.

Hospital Ship—I have absolutely no recollection of the trip.

Saipan—spent several days at this hospital in what I recall was the Section 8 Ward. A doctor suggested I write to my mother and assure her that I was still alive. Boarded a cargo plane with stretchers and flew to Kwajalein.

Honolulu—wandered about in a bathrobe and pajamas. Encountered the Second Platoon Sergeant who had been hit in the eye with a bullet on Okinawa. I didn't think he would make it. He seemed to be doing OK. I recall a doctor's comment, while I was there, "Every man has a breaking point when under the combat conditions to which we were subjected."

Wakeman Convalescent Hospital, Camp Atterbury, Indiana—given 30 day furlough—caught an old train and headed home. It had been over two years since I'd been able to return to the farm.

October 4, 1945—awarded an Honorable Medical discharge and Silver Star. When we were handed our medical discharges, the recruiting officer gave us a pep talk regarding the subject of "re-enlisting." It would appear that little attention had been given to the 'medical' aspects of our discharges.

VA follow-up checks on the medical discharge and the award of 50 percent disability:

1947—VA facility at Auburn
1947—VA facility at Stockton
1947—VA facility at Sacramento
194?—VA facility at Menlo Park
195?—VA facility at Salt Lake City
1961—Outpatient office visits with psychiatrist through 1972
1965—Reported for medical exam VAOPC, San Francisco
1972—VA facility at Martinez
1973—VA facility at Livermore
1988—Outpatient visits with Dr. D.

199?—Received "Purple Card" at the Sacramento Clinic
199?—Started monthly visits with Mental Health Technician

By dwelling on the past, you lose time in the present, but you develop, and maybe guarantee, a future for yourself that will be quite different from the past.

I've realized at 71 years, that I've been unaware of life. I have missed all that living and, finally, I'm beginning to realize why. I've searched for years to find that which I am, what I've missed, and why!

Is there time for tomorrow or should I just try to make it through each day? Maybe like they taught us in AA: One Day at a Time. That is fine if you do not hope for a future for you and your family because things should not remain as they have been.

I'm at a loss as to what to do. Now, 52 years later: It is quite late to make a start but there appears to be no alternative. I have not been able to obtain any satisfactory answers from the VA or from the OPM during all of my communications these past many years. I'm beginning to realize that if anything is to be done, it is up to me to initiate it and pursue it to a just conclusion.

How far from reality I've lived. Maybe it is the same as in combat.

YOU MUST NOT LIVE WITH REALITY.

We know that combat does carnage to the body. Can you quantify what it does to the mind of a young man, who cannot legally order a drink in a bar, but who has landed twice on an enemy beach, that was littered with dead men?

It is sad when young men lose so much so early. Before they can even appreciate what "young" is they returned (those who could) after the war, with no background, no idea how to fit in. They must go on ad-libbing normalcy and somehow survive.

Can they catch up? Or must they continue to be on the edge of a society that does not condone discussions of mental health or recognize the aberrations that have been caused by too much death and dying?

What is the damage to the human spirit, to the soul of the men or women?

The war is over for you. You are discharged. Back to civilian life: But how? You were never an adult civilian. You never even finished high school. You have no experience at a normal adult life; you never completed your teens, how do you start a grown-up's approach to an everyday, ordinary routine of living and thinking?

But for years you face the semi- and the sub-conscious aspects of stress and the pseudo-death qualities of your past horrors, although time does lessen some of the impacts. It is a long time before you have an inkling that maybe you are not like others, maybe not even normal. But with whom do you discuss such things? Who would understand?

You must continue. You must persevere.

Finally, now, you have gained a perspective: No one should ever have to do that. Only another front-line infantryman can understand what it is like. Face to face, hand to hand.

I faltered. I succumbed to the intensities of the strife, to the horrors of the mind.

Author's note: The 7th Infantry Division history on Okinawa records: "Total casualties suffered by the Division during the first ten days amounted to 1,119—120 killed, 696 injured, 13 missing, and 290 evacuated because of battle fatigue or as non-battle casualties." This 290 comprises 25.9 percent of the 1,119. Note the use of the phrase "battle fatigue." In 1945, the term was "nervous disability."

———

Perry Myers
Specialist/5, USA, 1st Air Cav Div,
Binh Long Province, Vietnam, 1968–1969

I've had four different shrinks tell me the best thing I could do for myself is to become involved in veterans organizations. Two years ago, I belonged to none. Now I'm a "life member" of three, and a yearly dues paying member of 13 more.

Okay, so big deal, right? Well, it works for me.

Sometimes it's painful to listen. Often it reminds me of things I'd like not to remember. But, it helps. It helps a lot.

The one message that seems to prevail is: We just gotta rebuild. We just gotta stay above it all. We gotta help each other so we can help ourselves.

I'm one of the lucky ones. I've got a good wife and three children. Sometimes it's pretty tough. Sometimes I get pretty down. Then I get mad and fight back. My way of fighting back is to not let it get me down. To rebuild. To focus on positive goals and thoughts and to set an example to other vets.

Hill 55

George Hill
Corporal, USMC, Vietnam, 1967–1969

The men I was with were unique, and from an 18-year-old's perspective, they were worldly and understanding of my being "a new guy."

In most cases, they were only a few years older than me, but they seemed so very wise. Through our combined efforts, we were able to survive in a very difficult time and place.

These Marines—Lt. Brown, Sgt. Green, Mac, and Rizzutto, among others—exemplified camaraderie and bravery at its finest. These men were so together and helped me through a lot of experiences that most people thankfully never come close to encountering.

Since 1970 I've had many difficult years, but throughout them all, these men were only a phone call away when I needed them.

They were always there with no questions asked, especially during the difficult years when even our government would not recognize or help with any of the post-Vietnam problems experienced by many.

I'm so glad most of these men's lives have been productive and they've really done well for themselves. I'm very thankful and proud of them.

The dead, as with the living, are my comrades to this day. There is no doubt that the dirt of that "Hill" still holds traces of the blood of Thuet, DeLano, Houser, and Baby Huey. These are Marines I knew. There were many others.

A person I talked to recently who had gone back to "55" said that although the hill was overgrown and water buffalo grazed, the trenches that we spent countless miserable nights in still deeply scar the hill's perimeter.

The Vietnamese had erected a stone monument for their sacrifices—everything for nothing except the real feeling of life and camaraderie gained, experienced, and never forgotten.

The brotherhood and feelings for a group of Marines, a place, and a time: If there was a word defining the feeling I've never heard of it.

Helping Hand

Charles Edward Elliott
Lance Corporal, USMC,
Dong Ha, Vietnam, 1967–1968

After leaving Vietnam
We all needed to find a helping hand
Someone, who would understand
The confusion in this man
After many years had passed
We found help, at last
Was it God's destiny, or fate
For us to find our way, to this place
Before, it was too late

For me, it began in West Palm Beach
I began to find some peace
At a place called the Vet Center
I began to believe I would be a winner
I met brothers who understood
Like no one else could

We had all been through the same thing
We all shared the same pain
We were not insane
We were not to blame
We reached out to each other

We are a family of brothers
A family for life
We survived the fight
Special thanks, to all the people at the Vet Center
Thank God, for your helping hand

Earl Z.
Sergeant, USMC, Vietnam

I had nowhere else to turn. I couldn't afford a psychiatrist, I was hesitant to talk to anyone anyway, because I thought I was the only one experiencing these problems. Having been in the war I figured that I was supposed to feel this way. In 1981 I went to the Vet Center. I told them what my problems were and said if they were unable to help me I was prepared to end my life. From that point on I began to understand that I wasn't the only one having these problems. I went "one-on-one" weekly. As I became more comfortable, I then attended group therapy ("group") once a week.

Having PTSD is a burden on me and my family. I still attend sessions and take anti-depressants to establish some sort of mental stability. I am still very angry. At times I cry for no reason. I try to deal with these emotions daily. Much of the time it is difficult to put these feelings aside and cope. Friends wonder why. The war was over for you in '69, why should you still feel this way, they ask?

The most helpful aspect of healing for me was group therapy. Although we had our share of GI Joes who talked more about combat than they really experienced, group gave me one opportunity to share with those who experienced many of the same things. I didn't feel alone anymore. Family members should get involved in their own groups. They need to understand why their spouses act the way they do, or why mom or dad is always angry and distant.

I still struggle every day to keep my emotions in check. But I feel by continuing to want to get better I can put these feelings in their place and go on with my life.

Ronald P.
Sergeant, USA, Vietnam, 1968

My unit arrived in R.V.N. on or about 1 Aug. 1968. We were attached to the 101st ABN. Div at Camp Eagle between Phu Bai and Hue. The unit designation was D troop 1st Sqdn. 1st Cav. Regt. We were Air Cav. We provided air reconnaissance for the Division Headquarters. The first two weeks or so were spent learning the area of operations in the division. In the beginning the crew consisted of two pilots and a gunner.

On 16 Aug. 1968 the platoon leader, one other pilot, and the platoon sergeant were on a local area recon when they were taken under fire by the enemy in a tree line. The platoon leader was killed and the platoon sergeant was wounded. The other pilot was able to keep the aircraft flying and get the wounded people to the hospital in Phu Bai. The LT was the first K.I.A. in the unit.

About two weeks later I was the gunner on a recon mission when we flew over a large group of people near a small village. We flew over this group when I spotted a person in the middle wearing a pith helmet. As we made a second pass over them this individual broke out of the crowd and started to run. He was dressed in khaki and had on leather web gear with a sidearm. As he was running the pilot positioned the helicopter so I would have a good shot at this person. I opened up with my M60 and cut him down. He was still moving, the gunship that was supplying air cover radioed for us to get out of the way because they were coming in hot. We moved to a position that we could watch what they were going to do.

The enemy soldier had just about crawled into a hooch when the gunship fired two rockets. When the smoke cleared, the hooch and soldier had disappeared. I was credited with the first kill for the unit. At the time it made me feel good that I had kind of evened the score with the enemy, never thinking that this incident would come back to haunt me years later. This is just one of many incidents that have troubled me.

What is it like having PTSD? It's like a dark cloud hanging over my head every day. What has it done to my family? My wife did not know how to handle my mood swings and she used to walk around me like she was walking on egg shells. My son never knew what kind of mood I was going to be in when he would get home from school; he would stay away from me as much as he could. I never physically abused either my wife or son. Mentally was a different story. Both of my families have paid a heavy price mentally from my not understanding what was happening to me. I was having thoughts of suicide when my present wife called the Vet Center and I got into counseling.

I feel that the combat trauma is not as bad now. Usually I can see what is happening to me before it gets out of hand. I see the world as a pretty good place to be now. I'm not ready to leave yet.

The thing that has helped me in my healing is having a counselor who understands what is happening in my life and who is able to give me suggestions on what to do. I have a hard time at certain dates or certain times of the year. I don't like to be around Fourth of July fireworks. August is a bad month for me; rain and humidity are "triggers" that I can now recognize. Being in therapy has helped me to see these things as triggers.

I hope this will be of some help to you. This is the first time that I have sat down and put these things on paper, so this has helped me in a way. I still have a problem with survivor's guilt but my therapist and I are working on it.

John J. Lennox
Staff Sergeant, USA, "A" Btry 10th Field Artillery Bn
3rd Inf Div, Korea, 1950-1951
Sergeant First Class, USA, 1099th Medium Boat Co Mobile Riverine Force,
Cat Lai, Mekong Delta, Vietnam, 1968-1969

I had been going to the Veterans Outreach Center in Rochester off and on since 1984. I felt I was getting some help, but no real breakthrough. It seemed as if the group was merely a rap session. Same old bullshit every week: war stories—can you top this one? Or we would sit around and curse Jane Fonda, "the bitch," or Richard Nixon, "the dirty bastard." Each week, the same stuff, over and over. The sad part is that a lot of guys don't want to go beyond pissing and moaning. I had to believe it's either because they enjoy feeling that life sucks and enjoy bitching, or they are scared to death to look inside and deal with what happened.

I was also going one-on-one with a wonderful counselor. My sessions with her were more helpful than the group therapy. With her I talked about some of my feelings, but still never let go of all the baggage. The point I'm making is that, in the beginning, the rap groups were good. They were a chance for vets who felt isolated from the public to let off steam with one another. But the real issues never got addressed

What are the real issues? We're pissed, we have nightmares and flashbacks. We feel guilt, shame, despair, maybe even suicidal. We find ourselves crying and don't know why. Life sucks. We sit in a corner of a restaurant facing the door. We drive to work on one route and take a different way home. The sound of a helicopter turns our stomachs into a blender; we don't want to look up, but we're helpless. Our eyes go skyward—what's its mission? A "dustoff" coming to haul away the dead, the wounded, or the ones who are going to die? Is it dumping us into a hot LZ? All I know is that I'm back in the bush. I have my hand on my head so the blade won't wash my bush hat away, but I'm not wearing a hat. When I smell smoke, it's a Zippo raid, burning villages. How those people must have hated us. I dreaded going to bed because I knew the nightmares would visit. I'd have felt safer in a foxhole.

There were so many things that haunted us, and we didn't know why. Or maybe we did know, but didn't want anyone else to find out. We didn't want to face these things.

In the June 1993 issue of "Rolling Stone," Paul Solotaroff wrote an article on a New England Shelter for Homeless Vets in Boston. Because my Rochester therapist was not available, I called the Boston PTSD specialist, George Mendoza, who invited my wife and me to visit. After speaking with him, I knew that he was a man who really cared.

The Boston program is a turning point for the vets. No rap or bitch sessions. You ask for help and they give it to you. When you walk in, you get searched. If you need detox, they send you to detox. Rules are simple: no booze, drugs, or weapons. You get a bed, clean clothes, and three meals a day. Everyone works to keep the center clean, and you *will* be on time for all counseling sessions and groups. They promise you that if you're serious about getting help, when you leave you'll have a job and a place to live. Break any of the rules and they show you the door. They don't mess with phonies, there are too many men waiting to get help who really want it.

George Mendoza spoke with my wife and me at length. His sincerity and concern brought tears to my eyes. I thought, "This man doesn't know us from Adam, and he really cares about us." His message was "There is *hope* for us all. Reach out for help—it's there." He made an appointment for me back home at the Rochester Vet Center, and I started one-on-one therapy with a new counselor. After a few months, he asked me to consider joining a group, and I've only missed one session since I started. My counselor and the group are dynamite.

It's been a long, slow process, and I'm grateful for the people and places that have been put in my path to lead me to where I am now. None of this would have been possible without Jesus Christ, my savior. Each day I get on my knees and thank Him for my blessings. I truly believe that my recovery has been through the grace of God. In *Out of the Night: The Spiritual Journey of Vietnam Vets*, William Mahedy calls recovery "the spiritual journey of Vietnam vets." Jesus said, "Apart from me, you can do nothing." I believe this with all my being.

Catherine M. Lennox
Wife of 32 years of Korean and Vietnam War Veteran

It is difficult to tell a short story, but I will concentrate on how I saw my husband affected by his experiences and the path we've taken toward recovery.

My husband left for Vietnam in November 1968. During his year In Country, he wrote to me nearly every day, which I now think is amazing. He never told me anything significant about the war, only superficial things—the weather, what he ate, and comments on my reports about the children. I cannot believe that I never realized at the time how he was covering up all the danger and horror he was experiencing.

I'd been warned to expect him to be different when he returned but I had no idea what this meant, nor did I expect anything but pure joy at his homecoming. He was exhausted and wanted no celebration, and the "Welcome Home" sign we made he quickly took down. He was appalled at the condition of our rented house, and insisted on moving the next day to our new duty station. My husband, who is an alcoholic, was in recovery prior to his tour. His Vietnam service interrupted his participation in support groups. He did not go back to drinking after his return, but had a few scary slips which brought him to A.A. now and then. He decided to leave the Army in 1970; for the next 14 years he never spoke of Vietnam to me. Only recently has he told me that he screamed or cried to himself in the basement or car and had nightmares constantly. He felt he was protecting me by keeping this secret.

In 1984, he took our three youngest children to a Memorial Day parade, and saw the local chapter of Vietnam Vets marching. A newspaper photographer saw that he was overcome with emotion. and the next morning his picture was on the front page. The local VVA saw the picture and contacted him; he joined the group and for the first time connected with other veterans.

The chapter was located in the same building as the Outreach Center, but John only went to see the counselor twice, until 1987 when, after a particularly stressful time, he experienced excruciating chest pain and collapsed. At first, we thought he was having a heart attack, but then discovered the problem was stress. A counselor from the Outreach Center visited him in the hospital and suggested he come see her, which he did sporadically for the next few years. It was a start.

I began to go to a weekly women's support group with the same counselor. I learn a lot from these meetings and from reading every memoir and biography I could find. They helped me understand what my husband had been hiding all these years and he began to share some of his experiences with me. One phenomenon that still amazes me is that after 20 years these memories still are impossible to contain. I now realize that stressors in your life can bring the memories out—that certainly was our experience. During these four or five years he attended rap group sessions; the friendships he made with these men were very helpful. They supported us in times of crisis; mostly giving understanding and love, as did our counselor.

John obtained a brochure, "Spiritual Steps for Combat Trauma," at the Outreach Center written by a psychiatrist, Dr. Joel Brende, and a Catholic priest, Father McDonald. We were able to meet Father McDonald, and spoke with Dr. Brende. Both men gave us hope when we needed it. We also read *Out of the Night: The Spiritual Journey of Vietnam Vets* by William P. Mahedy. I believe we were directed to all these men by a higher power.

John applied for disability for PTSD. It was a tedious process and we were not too hopeful. Due to a disability claim, a VA psychiatrist who was following John prescribed Valium, as did an internist when John was hospitalized with the stress attack. This was a disaster; my husband would never use mind-altering drugs, but how do you argue when you believe you have no choice?

In 1993, John's counselor wasn't available. I read a "Rolling Stone" article about George Mendoza in Boston, who was able to help vets without using drugs. I was very interested and made an appointment with him. John was in a very poor emotional state when we arrived in Boston, and anxious about the meeting. He was afraid of what he might be asked to reveal. I wondered if I would even be allowed inside, since it was a men's shelter but we were warmly received and given a complete tour. Words fail to tell how wonderful everyone was! John sat in on group sessions and we spent precious time with George, who made arrangements for follow-up with a counselor in our city. It was suggested John go to an out-of-state VA hospital for PTSD therapy, but he decided he could not afford this, and he did not want to go so far from home. Instead he went to the VA hospital in Buffalo for a three-day stay. It was traumatic, yet helpful, in that he saw so many suffering men there and he realized how lucky he was.

Since returning from Boston, John has joined the Vet Center's group sessions, which are valuable because they are small, structured, and no-nonsense. The camaraderie, wisdom, and insight he has obtained have helped him recognize and control the episodes of chest pain more than once. I also give credit to a hypnotherapist who taught us relaxation techniques which John has used alleviate the pain. (John has also used self-hypnosis to try to stop smoking, but that has not been so successful.)

George Mendoza stays in touch with letters and calls. We are grateful that we have people who really care about us and offer to help. Miraculously my husband has worked his way through episodes of chest pain, has fewer nightmares, and for the first time has had nights of complete rest.

Another major change, and example of God's help, is that John left his part-time job a few months ago. He had been a conscientious, hard worker all of his life—never complaining. This time he voiced his opinion and was told he could leave by a "horse's ass supervisor," and did just that—very quietly, never losing his cool. I was very proud of him, even though we were very concerned about our financial situation. That very afternoon, he got a letter from the VA awarding him 30% disability. That helped our financial problem, but even more, it made him feel that he was finally recognized by the government that had taken so long to give any recognition to his problem.

My husband is presently attempting to enroll in college to become a chemical dependency counselor. Our route was not straight, but thank God we persevered and finally know enough to see the light at the end of the tunnel.

Hopscotch

C. E. Orr

USN, In Country Combat Photographer, Vietnam, 1966–1968

I know an exit to madness just off I-5
It is called the Beacon Hilton, know where I mean?
The seventh floor is a land of deliriums
Seven east and seven west are where
the Vietnam Vet is put to the test

I park my chariot then hump up the hill
There to join my confederates also considered mentally ill
There's J. R., Rick, Haywire, Killer, and Doc Jim
Another clusterfuck I thought looking at them

To obtain service at this Hotel you must threaten harm to yourself
     or others
You could don propeller caps and wear hula-hoops
Yet remain invisible

Lurking in the hallways are Freudians and Jungians
All seem fascinated with our neuroses
It helps them forget their own
More than a few are bipolar crackpots or ghoulish wannabees

It is here the good doctors attempt Vietnam lobotomies
Their tools are hypnosis, group, and drug therapy
They do not know that both their and our psychoses are locked
     behind subconscious doors

We laugh at ourselves, try to find answers
Let's see who can climb the greased flagpole
Erected daily by the headshrinkers
To them we are nothing more than double-dealing March hares

Do you think you are special or something?
Why don't you get a job and get out of my hair!
They don't have to say it, it's in their eyes
I used to play hopscotch with "Fuck you" lizards

I was even known to dance with rock apes in the Nam
Today the shrinkers say Nam is the monkey
And it's he that is playing hopscotch with me

Treatment After Vietnam

Kellan Kyllo
USMC, HMM-162, Ky Ha, Marble Mountain,
Quang Tri, Vietnam, 1966–1968

The hospital staff surrounded him,
tied him down,
four leather straps,
then seven straps
and plenty of Thorazine
for days
until
the realness of enemy pictures
went away.

Clock Comments

Walter "Angus" Vieira
Corporal, USMC, SLF 9th MAB RLT 26 5th Marines,
Vietnam, 1967

It's two o'clock
and all is well.
The watchman said,
Now, go to hell.
Which way is that?
I asked with hate.
Just out your door.
Just past your gate.
Just one direction.
Just walk

straight.
How long will
it take
before I
arrive?
You'll always
be there.
As long as you're
alive.
It's three o'clock.
and all is well.
For one whole
hour
you've been in
hell.
Watchman, I don't
like your tone.
I've been in hell,
and so it's
true.
But I don't
need
to hear it from
you.
Man I wish
you'd go away.
Don't need your
mouth
Every hour of the
day.
Want me to go
away? I will.
But how will
you know
when to swallow
your
pills?
I just don't get
this connection

with hell.
And I'm lucky
I've got these
pills as well.
It's all very simple.
so easy to see
You really do
need me
to tell you
it's three.
You just don't
want to hear
my comments
thus far.
But don't swallow
your pills.
And you'll know
where you
are.
So, when I tell
you
it's three or it's
four.
Just swallow
your pills
or else
stay indoors.

Robert Aldrich
Sergeant, USA, 2/39th Inf 9th Div,
Vietnam, 1968–1969

I go to the doc'
To find some relief
Pills upon pills
It's beyond all belief.

All I can do
Is struggle through life
Hoping in vain
That I can beat this pain.

PTSD

C. E. Orr
USN, In Country Combat Photographer,
Vietnam, 1966–1968

PTSD, PTSD
Others may have it, possibly me

Now it begins, the losing of friends
Nightmares of Nam, a demon that grins

With bottled-up problems, you often explode
Feelings and senses begin to erode

Tell me, dear doctor, why is it best
To talk of dark things that cause me unrest

When finally you know me, surely you'll see
Inside this person, once there was me

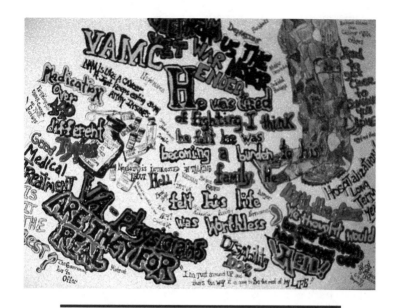

It's Hard to Get Close to Someone You Love

Sgt. Richard G. Lawrence
Combat Vietnam Veteran, USMC

"Medication and long-term therapy still do not guarantee anything."

A Feelin' on Healin'

Walter "Angus" Vieira
Corporal, USMC, SLF 9th, MAB RLT 26 5th Marines,
Vietnam, 1967

Me—I'm lookin for this healin'
I been hearin' about.
And my problem is that;
I just can't get out.
They say it's down south in the city of D.C.
But I got this paranoia
that keeps me you see

from travelin' out like most of the rest.
Perhaps I can send off for some
via U.P.S.
Gotta try to figure out this problem I got,
to get this healin' and me in the very same spot.
I picture me bein' there, fallin' down,
standin' tall.
Touchin' an feelin' this big black
marble wall.
An sobbin' an rememberin' an cryin'
an squealin.'
An grabbin' big chunks of this good
stuff called healin.'
Paranoia's been my friend and
my buddy for so long,
he's watched over and protected
me so nothin' goes wrong.
From the decade of the sixties,
all the way up until now,
An I'm supposed to turn around
and snuff him out now—somehow.
I want to and I don't, my
mind just keeps wheelin.'
But God I'm so starvin'
for that meal they call healin.'
I keep watchin,' an listenin' to these old
grunts—are they safe?
Before my old friend paranoia, I hit hard
and really waste.
I'm so puzzled an confused, by these cards
they been dealin,'
Yet their faces and their eyes show
they've really pigged on healin.'
I don't know, I don't know, I can't figure, I can't see
How in hell, I'm ever gonna,
get my ass to D.C.

To Emmett

Ed O.
Vietnam

His voice is cold as frozen snow,
Heavy with poison, lies.

Our sessions have become mere fencing matches.
His questions are sharp, stinging;
I parry them with simple truths.

Theory is his only weapon,
Mine is experience, reality.
He doesn't have a chance.

Had he stared, smelled, or spit in the face of
    death, I might allow him inside my wire . . .
He doesn't deserve to be there.

I view him with contempt and a strange pity,
Oftentimes I think of flushing that which
    contaminates my soul,
Give him what he feels he should know.

That would be too much shit,
He could not stay above it.
I chuckle at the thought.

Author's note: "This Jungian madman [the therapist] had a very real talent for
squeezing out nightmares, but could not deal with them after he had done so."

Rosemary A.
USA, Vietnam

I met a wonderful person who today remains a good friend, who told me that there was great sadness in my eyes. I had always thought they were OK eyes. He convinced me to talk with him . . . he was a VA counselor. My memories are so guarded that we do not get very far, but at least I know and understand why this is happening now, and seem better able to handle it. I have *never* told anyone about my experiences in VN, and will probably take them with me to the grave. If that makes me any less of a person, then so be it.

Harold James Glick
Corporal, USMC, An Hoa, Vietnam, 1968–1969

I served as a U.S. Marine in Vietnam from 1968-1969. I served 11 months and 20 days with the 5th Marine Infantry Regiment and six months on an M50 gun crew behind Freedom Hill, 3rd MP Battalion. I was honorably discharged.

I did not realize I had PTSD until March 1981. I was in the Ohio Army National Guard and when it came time for me to qualify with my weapon on the rifle range, I got sick, had the shakes, and almost had a flashback. I was taken to the Dayton VA. Upon release I was given a medical discharge under honorable conditions. I have been an outpatient at the Dayton VA and have had counseling at the Vietnam Vet Center since then. Anniversary dates give me problems with PTSD. Memorial Day is the worst, and before Christmas, and January 21-30 (I was in Liberty Bridge Battle in January 1969) are also difficult.

I am married (19 years) and have two kids. I have been employed by the government for 20 years and recently received a Bachelor of Science Degree in Business. I play guitar and write songs for a national record company.

You can lead a productive, happy, normal life with PTSD but you have to stay with Vet Center and VA Outpatient program. I take an antidepressant at bedtime.

Joe's Eyes

Jacqueline Garrick
Captain, USA, Medical Service Corps
Social worker (MSW, CSW, ACSW) specializing in PTSD treatment

I looked into his eyes,
and saw a war that is still being fought inside.
Pictures of injustice, destruction, and death
were still full of fire in those eyes.
He turned; looked away.
The sun passed through his hair, which flowed past his shoulders.
It grew as if it was a reminder of the years gone
since those innocent eyes were ravaged.
He sighs, exhales smoke, turns back.
I look again into those eyes
past violent battle scenes, deep hurt, and a raging anger.
And from those same eyes,
I learn a code of honor, and of a bond that can exist
between human beings.
I feel the intensity of those eyes radiating within me.
All my energy is focused with him.
He then begins to speak from beyond those eyes.

The Counselor's Two Way Street

Frank-Josip Racic
Sergeant, USA, Vietnam, 1968–1970

He came into my office just like countless other
Veterans before him have, wanting one thing;
desperately needing another.

Wearing his pain better than most, neatly pressed
without wrinkle, like his plaid shirt or his ageless
face, he began to slowly open up.

When I asked him how I could help, his
countenance changed remarkably as his voice drifted
down an octave lower.

He then began to lay out his life; a series of failed
relationships, broken dreams, and shattered hopes for a
brighter tomorrow.

Listening to him relate how it has been; some of my own
readjustment experiences became vividly portrayed in
his fragmented words.

Many of my old frustrations were personified, and I
could only imagine the pain of having to live through
feeling them again.

As he talked, I directed the conversation to how it was
and what it was like for him before it all seemed to
fall apart.

His concern was his inability to have a deep and
meaningful lasting relationship with a significant
other since he lost a friend to an enemy bullet.

I was surprised that he never mentioned having
been awarded the Bronze Star for volunteering to go in
and rescue a downed Medevac chopper either.

When I asked him about his Bronze Star he began to
evade me saying, "Someone had to go in and get them
out . . . ." Now it was my turn to go in and do the same.

Therapy Session

Cheryl P. Burrows
Wife of Vietnam Veteran

Blank stares.
Seems like you are thousands of miles away.
It was so long ago, but not for you.

Rice paddies.
A firefight.
The elderly Vietnamese and children.
Bury the dead.
A survivor.

Weeping.
Transfixed.
Talk of the crucifixion and Pope John.
Tears and holding each other.
I'm the observer while the medicine man works.

Exorcism and magic.
Forgiveness and healing.
Reality.
You can leave the rice paddies and come home.

Stress Under Management

Walter "Angus" Vieira
Corporal, USMC, SLF 9th , MAB RLT 26 5th Marines,
Vietnam, 1967

"Sit down right
under the fluorescent light.
Try and squeeze
your muscles tight.
Take a deep
breath.

Hold it please.
With both hands,
grab both knees.
When I say 'Now,'
pucker your lips.
Blow out the air,
tighten your hips.
Grab a chair,
hold it high.
Right index finger
in left eye."
All good intentions,
taken well.
I'm real relaxed,
confused as hell.
"In here we teach
relaxing, see?
For help with
confusion,
down the hall.
Room 2B."
"Miss, there's 84
men
in the confusion
line."
"I'd like to wait
but I don't
have the time.
My meter's
expired.
I ain't got
a dime.
And I noticed
I've been speaking.
only in rhyme."
"Then confusion isn't
what you want.
Get in the rhyme line,
it's real short."
Too much, rhyming man.

I said
one thing,
no, two.
He said roses are red
and violets are blue.
"I'm startin' to feel
real upset and
uptight."
"You'd better get
under a fluorescent light."

4

DESPAIR

"Would tell you who I am . . .
If I knew . . .
Would tell you how I felt . . .
If I could feel . . ."
Rosemary A.

The despair endured by combat veterans haunts them both before and during treatment for traumatic stress. Male veterans are tortured by the pointman who "got it" on patrol, women by the pain and suffering they witnessed in the MASHs and Evacs; both are burdened by the responsibility they once had—to fight for life in the face of death. They despair the war's continuing effect on their lives and their families' lives, their inability to feel, to function, and to contribute.

During therapy, the sense of despair can deepen as veterans relive the past and touch what they see as lost hopes and shattered dreams. They view themselves as "broken"; some cannot see, and others appear not to want to learn how they can be made whole. Often they question why they began therapy at all, since periodic counseling sessions or daily medication only seem to prolong their suffering or reveal greater pain instead of providing the healing they seek.

But a man or woman can only despair if he or she has once known hope, had aspirations, or felt a personal peace with the world and with him- or herself. It is the loss of hope, the sense that things will never be the same, and that peace is beyond their control that leads to despair. To some, despair is a barrier to retrieving who (and what) they have been. Frustrated by the slow course of therapy, the pursuit of dead ends, reliance on medications, and a seemingly indifferent "system," the vets' challenge is to learn who they are, rediscover the sense of hope they once knew, and find peace.

Invisible Wounds of War

Sgt. Richard G. Lawrence
Combat Vietnam Veteran, USMC

"You don't get a Purple Heart for these wounds.
The wound is embedded in your mind."

George "Argo" Jackson
Sergeant, USMC, 1st Marine Air Wing,
I-Corps, Vietnam, 1967–1970

Take a young man from a small country town, where the big deal is to sit next to the pot belly stove and hear about the big one that got away, or how the big war was won and this police action in Vietnam is child's play. Send him to boot camp, train him how to survive all things by killing whatever gets in his way, or slows him down. Train his mind to do whatever it takes. Send him off to war where nothing he has learned helps overcome that first night in combat. To kill first, ask questions later. Have him crawl across body parts that were once his friends, shoot him, expose him to drugs, and when he has a problem, tell him everyone is going through the same thing, and he'll get over it. Have him kill his own, let him think this can happen to him too. Let him see people die daily, then be a good Marine, and do it all over again. Bring him home to a world where he had better wear something besides the uniform he has become proud of and give him medals that will not get him a cup of coffee. Let his friends in the world call him "Baby Killer" and the police take him to jail for beating the shit out of someone who just threw piss or shit on him. Tell him life will get better; 20 years later he still waits. Have his parents say, "I don't even know this old man that my 20-year-old son has become, and I don't want to." Let him waste his life, trying to just get by, watch as his wife marries his best friend, because he forgot how to love or be part of a loving relationship. Ask him to trust someone, let him hear "I understand" one more time. Ask him why he lives alone, sleeps with a gun, has dreams of leaving someone behind, why life does not seem important, why he thinks there is no God. Call him crazy for caring about POW/MIAs and not being able to talk to anyone unless he has been In Country. Let him spend 20 years as a drug addict. Tell him it's because he likes to get high, as you watch him die from the inside. When he asks for help tell him to wait, there is no room for him. Then, 20-years-too-damn late, some s.o.b. calls it PTSD. Where were you when we needed you? Now you want to ask me to help you write a fucking moneymaking book for your damn glory. Welcome home.

Dana S.
1st Lieutenant, USA Nurse Corps, Vietnam

Therapy is a bitch. I'd rather go to the dentist and the gynecologist in the same day than go to therapy. But somehow I always manage to show up. My therapist started by asking for a complete run-down on my Army service and my tours in Vietnam. A snap, I thought—I don't even remember most of it! Well, during the 50-minute therapy session, I could usually cope fairly well, but afterwards was a different story. On the way home or in the middle of the night, I'd remember something that would really devastate me, and I'd have to carry it around alone for an entire week. If I tried to talk to my husband about it, he'd either change the subject as soon as possible or ply me with platitudes ("It wasn't your fault," "You did the best you could," "The past is past. . .").

For a while I thought that therapy was making me worse. For several days after a session I would have nightmares, flashbacks, and black moods seemingly worse than before. It reminded me of chemotherapy: as soon as I got around to feeling a little stronger, it was time for another dose.

But I stuck with it. I figured that if I was dragging up that much repressed putrefaction, ultimately I would be healthier. Although inelegant, the medical dictum "Pus and piss must come out" nevertheless remains true.

Attack

Charles Felix
Corporal, USMC, W.W. II:
Bougainville, Guam, Iwo Jima

Have you ever waited at daybreak?
Stretched in the muck and mire.
With your guts a throbbing ache,
And strained your tired eyes, red as fire.

Have you heard the sibilant whisper?
That warns of the approaching hour.
And fit the cold, cold bayonet,
For the dreadful chore ahead.

O God, have you known such fear?
Fear so frighteningly deep.
That the putrid vomit of dread,
Comes straining though clenched teeth.

Then clawing over the moldering bags,
Into the tearing wire.
Screaming through the murky jungle hell,
Teenage warriors, killers for hire.

And the comrades you left behind.
Remember them in the mud and wire.
They can never tell now,
Did it pain to die?

I can't tell you how,
For youth's song was never sung for them.
I don't know their pain either,
For I never died before.

Old Killers

Anonymous
Lance Corporal, USMC, Vietnam

I hide my young eyes in the VFW
they want my bullets and food
to hell with the beer
I hide my mind in the VFW
ancient killers lurk
hawking old gold Jap teeth
pulled from scarred memories
flies swarm in their eyes
feasting on Vietnamese blood
still wet on my hands
as I die in a Miller Light
The gooks are coming
they hiss in my ear
you can't kill the memories boy
fess up that ear you took
I threw it away I scream
then get out of here
the Krauts are coming

Hitting Bottom

Dennis R. Tenety
Lance Corporal, USMC (Ret), 1st Marine Division
India Co 1st Plt 3rd Bn 5th Reg, An Hoa, Vietnam, 1969

What a fucking mess I've made of things, and other people's lives! I haven't touched her lovingly—never not once. I've only treated her like shit. For once in all of these years, I thought I'd open up to someone special. I can't even do that! Here's someone so young. Someone who deserves better than the shit I've been putting her through. I've never realized what I've been like all these years. She has made me realize what a Fuck I've been. To say I'm sorry is not good enough. There will never be any words kind enough to undo my doings. I have been thinking a lot about it and now I think there is only one answer. I don't want to be in a hospital or do any more time.

I sit and wonder why I wasn't killed on that day, August 13, 1969. Now I know, I fucked that up too. I am fighting something I can't deal with and it has to come to an end. Why not? The rest of me stopped living on that day. It just took me this long to figure it out. My mind, soul, heart, and everything else I had bled out of me in that paddy in a place called Arizona. There's nothing but a body here today. Jim, I've been thinking maybe I'll join you and the others, wherever you are. If I do meet up with you, don't be pissed I took the cheap way out. Believe me, this is one war I can't handle. I don't know. I have to think. I have to find some way to tell my wife that I'm sorry for all my wrongs. I don't know what to say anymore. Fuck it all!

Existing

Rosemary A.
USA, Vietnam

Sanity is knowing you are
insane.
Insanity is refusing to feel pain,
Pain is simply being alive.
Living is knowing who you are

Would tell you who I am . . .
   If I knew . . .
Would tell you how I felt . . .
   If I could feel . . .

────

Dana S.
1st Lieutenant, USA Nurse Corps, Vietnam

For me the most difficult part of being a woman Vietnam veteran with PTSD has been the unremitting sense of isolation. After returning from Vietnam and leaving the Army, I simply didn't encounter any other women who had been in Vietnam. I thought my feelings were unique. Trying to be just like everyone else seemed to be the culturally accepted and expected thing to do; it was the only way to re-enter society and try to have a life after Vietnam. It was the only way to escape the vilification that was being endured by my brother veterans.

Over the years I was afraid to contact other nurses I had known in Vietnam. In the first place, the sense of camaraderie we had felt hadn't been about dissecting our emotions with each other, it had been about working as a team, being able to count on each other absolutely. What if they rebuffed me and didn't want to talk? What if they were worse off than I? What if I was the only one who hadn't merely resumed her prewar life? Those conflicting but equally depressing possibilities made reaching out too risky. Male veterans either didn't recognize me as a real veteran or assumed they already knew what my war had been like. They were willing to joke about the *nuoc mam*, the jungle rot, and the Saigon tea, but they weren't willing to exhume the pain. I felt only partially connected to them: We shared the same esoteric vocabulary and arcane geography, but it seemed we didn't share the same emotional terrain. They knew how it felt to kill the enemy with a gun, but they didn't know how it felt to kill one of our own with a syringe or simply by running out of time. They knew how it felt to see a buddy maimed by a booby trap; they didn't know how it felt to look into the eyes above the mangled legs and tell that buddy he would never walk again. They had nightmares about being overrun; they didn't have nightmares of crying out, "I'm wounded, too!" to male medics who never heard.

Likewise, society's silence about the war strangled me emotionally. I found that members of the Vietnam generation were expected to be either baby killers or war protesters. I had been neither. There was no niche in anybody's mental cupboard for whatever I was. Even when PTSD became the diagnosis of the month and Vietnam became a fit topic of conversation in polite circles, I was still invisible. Veterans were invariable referred to as "he" or "the men" or "troops"—at one of the newly-opened Vet Centers, I was politely informed that women don't develop PTSD. If I wasn't a real veteran, then I couldn't possibly suffer any real consequences of the war.

The irony of my situation is that through my attempts to deal with PTSD I have, in fact, met some quality people who are willing to reach out to me in my pain; yet the PTSD compels me to keep them at a distance. Ever since Vietnam I've been wary of letting anyone get too close. I feel like a runner caught between bases—I want only to be safe, but I am expending all my energy getting nowhere, just trying to escape being tagged out. I can't ever get back where I started, much less make any forward progress. My dilemma is, I believe, common in Vietnam vets. I believe my ultimate healing from the trauma of the war will be found in reconnecting to the human family, but my trauma itself lies partly in the rejection I experienced, and causes me to flee all connection. I complain bitterly about the isolation, yet sometimes the only comfort I am able to tolerate is the silent companionship of my cats.

I often feel that there is no one out there like me, no one with whom I can experience that wordless, intuitive kind of sharing that to me connotes true intimacy and understanding. The war and its aftermath have left me stranded between the past and the present. The war diminished my possibilities for growth as a person. I sense that I have a lesser future than I would have had had I not gone. I don't even fully remember what kind of person I was before Vietnam. What kind of person am I now? Can I ever be a whole person again? The war took something important from me, but I can't even define it, much less begin to get it back.

My PTSD and Me

Barry McC.
Master Sergeant, USMC, Vietnam

From a trauma in my life
That's buried deep in my head
Came my PTSD, my future in dread.

It festered and boiled then began to lash out
It made me hurt everyone I cared about
Lost my friends, my family, my children too
Please help me Lord, I know not what to do.

Is there some way Lord, you can take this from me?
Those I hurt will not forgive or forget, you see
Go from job to job, even land in jail
Sleeping in the streets is just pure hell.

Never knowing when my next attack may be
I'm always afraid to be part of society.
Who can help or even cares?
I've got nothing but my own nightmares.

Maybe some day they'll find a cure
Then in our sub-conscious we can unlock the door.
But for right now as you can see
I still have my old friend, my PTSD and me.

George W. Buck, Jr.
CWO II, USA, Pilot, 336th Assault
Helicopter Co, Soc Trang,
Vietnam, 1970

I,
X-Chief Warrant Officer II,
Helicopter pilot
Combat decorated—too late—
   over a year
   after my honorable
   discharge,
george william buck, jr.
Have decided to die at this
   wall
Near my friends
Because
I cannot endure
The continuing pains
Of injustice
Of disrespect
Of nightmares
Of alienation
And the fruitless efforts of
   trying again
And again
And again
In vain,
To realize
And to experience
The "answers"
That are supposed to bring
   inner peace.
My name may not be on this
   wall
But I am with those who
   physically died
   in Vietnam.
I died there emotionally,

Success

"To laugh often and love
   much;
to win the respect of intelligent
persons and the affection of
   children;
to earn the approbation of
   honest
citizens and endure the
   betrayal of
false friends;
   to appreciate beauty;
to find the best in others;
   to give of
one's self;
   to leave the world a bit
better, whether by a
   healthy child,
a garden patch or a redeemed
   social
condition; to have played
   and laughed
with enthusiasm and sung with

My physical death simply took
   longer,
As is the truth of the deaths of
   that greater
   number of fallen soldiers,
Than this wall reflects,
Who have died since that war.
There ought to be a memorial
For those of us who gave our
   best
But found it impossible to
   survive
To that happy old age.
We fought and died
So that you could have
That experience.
I have left this world a bit
   better for my efforts
And if this touches you
My "success" continues.

Summer 1992, 12 to 6 a.m.

Editors' note: The author survived
   to submit this in 1994.

exultation; *to know even*
   one life
has breathed easier because
   you have
Lived—this is to have
   succeeded."

Ralph Waldo Emerson
(Phrases in italic were marked by
George W. Buck, Jr.)

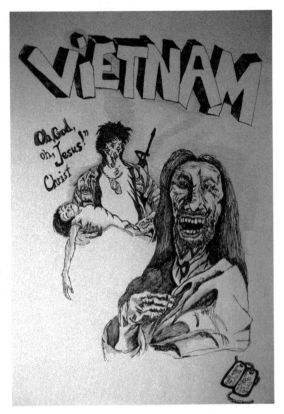

Where Was God?

Sgt. Richard G. Lawrence
Combat Vietnam Veteran,
USMC

"God is supposed to
protect you. Dead
bodies, missing arms,
legs. Where was God
in Vietnam?"

Eights and Aces

Dennis R. Tenety
Lance Corporal, USMC (Ret), 1st Marine Division
India Co 1st Plt 3rd Bn 5th Reg, An Hoa, Vietnam, 1969

To the hounds of Bastardville—you bent my mind on Devil's Island.
The crazies you weeded out, keeping only the insane. After seven
months, the only words that would stir my soul were *kill, gung ho,
Semper Fi*. Some of us learned all too well, always striving for the perfect kill.

Till this day, those same words stir the soul. The shattered mind
replays the battles that rule every second of my life. Visions, sounds,
odors are all it takes to set the hands of time to the past.

I want to work. I did at one time. I want to live another life for a day—without hate and rage. I want to be able to wake one dawn not wondering, "Why me?"

My emptiness is my own. I can't pass that off on anyone but myself. You don't bet on a "Dead man's hand."

———

Clyde Q.
Corporal, USMC (R),
South Korea, 1950–1951

For the past three years, save for my medication Doxepin and Clonazepam, I cannot sleep at night. My wife understands my condition and gives me moral support. *But will it ever stop?*

The horrible past has raised its ugly head. Now I live in painful memories. Each day I ask myself, *how much longer will it last*? My only solace is God, my wife, and my VA psychiatrist.

———

PTSD

Jerry T.
E-4, USA, 4th Inf Div, Vietnam

Now at 42, 43, and 44 years of age,
I feel like an animal locked in a cage.
Divorced, no friends, and a broken home,
"All I want" is to be left alone.
"Nothing wrong with you, forget about it."
I am tired of hearing these lies.
Then why, by our own hands, have so many died?
Some of us didn't make it; May their souls rest in peace.
The ones who are alive, are slowly killing themselves . . . .
    Thanks to You, PTSD

Disability Morning

Edward J. Burris
Vietnam

Sweeney rises
From the restless chloral hydrate sleep
Shuffles to the coffee maker
Begins the day.
ADLs done and dressed
Morning news
Cigarette
Coffee
What now
What next?
Sweeney's mind must be busy
Or he bedeviled
Sweeney's ghosts are never gone
But hover not helpful.
Daily walks
Among the strangers
Not strolling
Sweeney never secure
Never again.
Still this day
Still tomorrow
Poverty
Boredom
Slowly Sweeney
Disintegrates.
With this knowledge
Some of Sweeney
(The old soldier?)
Rebels
And reaches to that inner door
Of oblivion.
Sweeney strives to honor
The Brenda promise
The contract.

But
What now?
What next?
For Sweeney?
Disabled
In the morning.

The Vietnam Veteran Experience

George W. Buck, Jr.
CWO II, USA, Pilot, 336th Assault Helicopter Co,
Soc Trang, Vietnam, 1970

Nearly 23 years
After my tour in
Vietnam, This
picture reflects
In part, my experiences
Of both my time over there
And the years since,
As well as what the future
Looks like. Neither 100,000
Words nor 100,000 prayers
Have even begun to ease the anguish.
There should be no wonder why more of us
Vietnam vets have died since that war than the
Total number who died during the war; over three times as many.
What answers will eliminate this aftermath of anguish?
I have tried everything to no avail and now "they" want
To keep me on drugs again. The drugs make me feel
Weak, incapable of absolutely everything and severely
Vulnerable.
This is no way to live; There is no way to live. I'm sure
I'll go to heaven because I've spent my time in hell.
And it continues.

A Hard Sentence

Kellan Kyllo
USMC, HMM-162, Ky Ha, Marble Mountain,
Quang Tri, Vietnam, 1966–1968

He lived daily with friends whose lives
were threatened
with wounds
of death,
violent
month after month after month,
until his brain chemistry
denied
any more friendships.
as
long as he lived.

Roger McG.
E-4, USA, Vietnam

PTSD means the lasting stress after the exposure. I was a HU-1B helicopter crew-chief and saw combat in many forms, was wounded twice, lost many good friends. Four V.A. doctors have diagnosed me as having PTSD, and I am 50 percent compensated.

I have not been steadily employed for ten years. My wife and children did not understand. My wife was having an affair with a draft-dodger who fled to Canada. That really got to me! There was a lot of emotional and physical abuse in our marriage, so we separated.

Left my job at the U.S. Post Office, lost my house, and two beautiful children. Right now I am homeless and live in the bush next to a freeway. Have been in and out of the V.A. and other programs. Feel frustrated and lack hope. Have chronic depression, flashbacks, and bouts of anger. Would like to change but don't know how. Have problems with alcohol and sometimes drugs. There have been problems with the law. Have read much about this condition, but haven't got much valuable help.

Broken

Walter "Angus" Vieira
Corporal, USMC, SLF 9th MAB RLT 26 5th Marines,
Vietnam, 1967

Broken—
I don't wanna
be.
Broken—
Just ain't right
for
me.
Broken—
Ain't the way
to be.
Broken—
I ain't got
the
key.
Broken—
Ain't the way
to
be.
Broken—
I can't look
or see.
Broken—
Ain't no trip
for me.
Broken hearts,
broken
fences,
broken bottles,
undug
trenches.
No promise
spoken,
promises
unbroken.

Only
breakable
things—
can be
broken.
Offered words,
two cent
token.
Live it
busted,
live it
broken.
This world's
too heavy,
I ain't joken.
Can't get
patched up—
man
I been
broken.
Broken
stitches,
hearts' torn
open.
Hearts a' bleedin,
hearts been
broken.
Broken cane
in the pourin'
rain.
Standin' broken,
slip and fall.
Broken
man.
unbroken
Wall.
Pack the
bags.
Walk, run
or crawl.

Go get
fixed
at the wailing
wall.
Leave unbroken,
one and all.
Politician,
sits and
dreams.
Self-satisfied,
or so he
seems.
Awaitin' debts
long since
unpaid.
Find a page
and go get
laid.
Homeless lady,
man, and
child.
Life is good—
the winter's
mild.
Find a can,
turn it
in.
Get a nickel,
pleasure
within.
Broken lady.
Broken man.
Broken kids
who need a
hand.
Broken telescope
up there.
Two billion
dollars—
cheap repair

Politician,
head up
high,
fixed the telescope.
In the
sky.
Broken vet
needs a
pill.
Charge two
bucks.
Mail a
bill.
Broken Vet,
foul words
said.
Broken cop
cracks his
head.
Too many things,
all can't be
spoken.
Look real good.
Everything is
broken.
Broken cars.
Broken dreams.
Broken hope,
so it seems.
You and me
Ride the T.
Broken,
I don't wanna
be.

Broken God,
upon the tree,
perk one ear,
hear my plea.
Don't waste time

partin' big red seas.
Fix us up.
We're broken—
please.

Earl Z.
Sergeant, USMC, Vietnam

Something happened to me over there,
since then I've struggled with anger, desperation, and despair.

I was brought up believing in God, my Country,
and to respect my neighbor,

Now it seems I'm only worthy if I
do them a favor.

I volunteered for Vietnam and served
with pride,

For these past many years all I want
to do is hide.

I'm afraid of everything and I've a deep
distrust of all,

I've wished so many times that I was one
of those on The Wall.

Everyday is a constant struggle to survive,
I've worked my ass off to do a good job, but they
never seemed satisfied.

I wish I could end it all and commit
suicide,

But I haven't the courage to do it,
besides I think I've already died.

Maybe someday I again can become
something worthwhile,

Until then I can only wonder
how hard the next mile.

Thomas N. "Tommy" Bills
Sergeant, USA, 2/7th Cav (Gary Owen Bde) 1st Cav Div,
Vietnam, 1965–1966

I found losses from my childhood that I had either consciously or sub-consciously repressed. I found and grieved over a loss of childhood in-nocence, a loss of that beautiful time that could have been—growing from a boy to a man!

On Clarendon

Edward J. Burris
Vietnam

The withered bricks
Outside my window
Comprise the vista
Of my view
What has not
Been taken from me
I have cast away
In bloody guilt
Leaving withered bricks
For my eyes
Leaving bitter ashes
For my mouth.

Boy In A Box

John Malick
E-5, USA, 101st Airborne TDY 197th Trans.,
Vietnam, 1970–1972

At the end of an alley
down by the Saigon Bar
there was a box
small, and brown, dirty, and damp . . .

With eyes as dark as midnight
you looked up at me
without saying a word
you extended frail hand
small fingers upturned, pleading for help
I, the uncaring man
turned, and walked away . . .

Now I have returned
looking for a way out,
but you the unforgiving,
had moved on, box in tow . . .

If I were to find you
draped in your tattered clothes
would you forgive me
or will I carry your memory,
with me, for the rest of my days . . .

Two Children at My Loc

Ken Sauvage
Corporal, USMC, 2nd Bn 3rd
Marines, Vietnam,
1968–1969

"I don't feel bad about
what I did in the war, but I
do feel bad about what the
war did to the children."

Dana S.
1st Lieutenant, USA Nurse Corps, Vietnam

A wide sea separates
Home from Vietnam
laughter from mourning
purity from putrescence
what I was from what I cannot be

I falter at the edge of that ocean
with its Oriental dragons
swimming in blood

swallowing futures
stealing sleep
slaughtering love

My reincarnated Nachshon beckons
willing to show me across
but I've seen hands
vaporized
charred
macerated
I am wary of friendly fire
and I don't want to be
responsible
for anything
good
or bad
ever
again

5

LOSS, MOURNING, AND GRIEVING

"You missed life, my friend.
And I remember still in my own quiet hours,
Thinking that you deserved better,
And thanking you again for my life.
I still weep for you, if that can help."
Charles Felix

A soldier's death impacts those who knew him like the dropping of a stone into a lake. Spouse, parent, and child, brother and sister, friend or buddy feel the loss throughout their lives. They grieve for the soldier's absence, and for what he is missing as he would have aged: marriage, children, a satisfying career. Combat buddies are haunted by the death of a close friend in their unit and re-experience their memories sharply even into their elder years. Older veterans, as they lose their lifelong support system of spouse and friends, begin to display the symptoms of combat trauma.

Vets' writings reflect loss, mourning, and grief. Some vets consciously or unconsciously search for old friends, knowing neither if they are dead or alive, only that they are gone. Others numb themselves to the pain not permitting themselves to "feel" their sorrow.

Every veteran mourns a buddy, and every family member mourns a loved one. All the survivor has is the memory of that friend or loved one. Mourning keeps the lost veteran "immediate" and "alive." Many survivors see this as their duty to the dead and fear that if they "let go" of the memory, they will lose their only connection with their friend. Survival guilt can persist for many years, the survivor ever questioning and denying his own right to live. The memories are exacting and draining, and mourning can last a lifetime.

Grieving veterans write of the lost soldier being called home to God, or existing in the company of their fellows in the "hallowed silence" of Arlington National Cemetery, or on the Wall. Rather than letting go of the lost, the memory is spiritually transferred to another place, where both the survivor and the fallen warrior are at peace.

Marines

Sgt. Richard G. Lawrence
Combat Vietnam Veteran,
USMC

"Tom will always be in my
mind, forever."

Fallen Comrade

Charles Felix
Corporal, USMC, W.W. II:
Bougainville, Guam, Iwo Jima

I still weep for you,
And often in the lonely watch of the night,
I awaken and listen again to the jungle sounds,
And hear again the gentle lap of ocean beaches.

And I remember how it was before you died.

Soft, quiet dawn with brave men.
The sweet smell of morning as we went into battle.
Rank cordite smell and the stench of death,
With finally the tired and peaceful rest of victory.

But above all I weep for the memories you sacrificed.

I mourn for those experiences you never had.
Lovely autumn on a fun-filled campus,
And spring filled with a woman's love.
Children, and the very essence of life.
O, but you missed the challenges and sweet success of life.

You missed life my friend.

Yes, you missed all of these, oh comrade of mine.
And I remember still in my own quiet hours,
Thinking that you deserved better,
And thanking you again for my life.

And I still weep for you, if that can help.

Author's note: It was especially difficult to lose replacements only a few
months out of boot camp. I don't want to forget the comrades who died.

Monsoon Rains

Frank-Josip Racic
Sergeant, USA, Vietnam, 1968–1970

In dreams he keeps seeing children wandering in the
streets. Doesn't anybody care that they have no food
to eat? Doesn't anybody wonder why they have no place
to sleep? And there ain't enough in a monsoon rain.

To wash away all their sorrows and the shame and . . .
There ain't enough in a monsoon rain to wash away Agent
Orange and its stain. There ain't enough!

When Johnny became a soldier and was sent to Vietnam,
there he loved an Asian woman but then left her with

his son who walks the streets of Saigon searching for a
home and there ain't enough.

Since Johnny's back at home he's often feeling down
for things he did and saw when he was in Vietnam,
his life's had little meaning like his Amerasian son's.

In dreams he keeps seeing children crying in the
streets. Doesn't anybody wonder why they beg for food
to eat? Doesn't anybody care that they have no place to
sleep? And there ain't enough!

The Days of Old Henry's Death

Anonymous
Lance Corporal, USMC, Vietnam

Always a mournful look on your face
even with your intestines hanging out
gaunt sunken brown eyes
I can still hate you sometimes for dying on us
if I try.
Your Arkansas farm fields have long gone to weeds, Henry.
What's the use in trying anymore?
You carried your mother's picture
and the gooks splattered your blood on her face.
I couldn't bear to see the tired sad eyes
from which you sprang,
so I never went to tell your Ma how you died.
Could I tell her gallant lies?
We tried to keep the booze from you
(You always cried when you were drunk.)
Your fatalism kept us brave—
you scared us standing up in fire fights,
froth and hysterical laughter spewing forth
like your venomous bullets
old killer.
I was too fucked up to tell you to try to survive.

By the way,
Teddy caught a round in the head,
Mike killed himself in 1974,
and I still don't know where I am.

Moving Wall

Walter "Angus" Vieira
Corporal, USMC, SLF 9th MAB RLT 26 5th Marines,
Vietnam, 1967

Hey man, guess what
your name is in town.

It's carved in bold
letters
planted firm in the ground.

So many will see it
But sad as it is
They won't know who you
are
where you were
what you did

From what I can see
I'm the only one
around
who knew you
and loved you
'fore your name came to town.

Yeah, many will see it
lookin' up
walkin' round
but won't remember you
after
your name has left town.

And I wanna try to tell it
real relaxed and real calm
How it was
on the day
in a bag
you left
Nam.
A few guys threw you, in a stack
of five others.
All of 'em; beautiful people
every one of 'em brothers.
I didn't know you were
there
In that stack
on that day
when the choppers
came in
and they took you
away.
Then early that
night
long after that fight
someone mentioned the
fact.
That you were
medivaced.
"How bad was he
hit?"
I asked right
away
He just shook his
head
"No man, K.I.A."
when I heard them
words
I started to shake
My stomach got
sick
All night,
stayed awake.

It hasn't stopped
yet; these twenty-six years
Wrote about it in a poem.
"My eyes full o' tears."
They sent me home
too
not long after
you
The war ended without
glory
The rest
a long story
So here we are now
All those years; so much
later
And I'm seein you again
Man, what could be
greater?

But man, it could never
ever be quite the same
All I get to do now
Is look at your name.

But just think, my good
buddy
And take pride, and feel
real tall
Cause while the wall's
here in town
Your name's most loved
of all.

"Hei', dozo, buckatarni, meezo!
    Yeah, Yeah, Yeah."

Editors' note: The words are Japanese: "Yes, please, stupid, rain!"
Made-up "lyrics" the author and friends attempted to sing in
exchange for drinks on Okinawa.

Spirit of the Corps

Joel D.
Gunnery Sergeant, USMC,
Vietnam, 1966–1968, 1970

In the evening of my days,
And the silence of my thoughts,
I return to the spirit of the Corps,
I remain only a batted eyelash away from,
Parris Island, Chu Lai, Tam Ky, and Khe Lank.
The sounds of battle I will forever carry within,
Often frustration, fear, and anxiety rush in,
Where the spirit of my fellow Marines have been.
The battles have long since been over,
But in the evening of my days,
If only for a few moments . . .
I return in the silence of my thoughts,
To pay my respects,
To the final roll call,
Of my last battle,
I see each face and hear each voice,
And respectfully remember,
My fellow Marines,
Who fought with me and died,
Where only God,
The angels that carried their spirits,
And we survivors,
Know their acts of courage and personal sacrifice,
These men are the spirit of the Corps,
The Few, The Proud, The Marines.

Leading All the Way

Gregory Schlieve
Sergeant, USA, Co C 5/7 1st Air Cav Div,
Vietnam, 1969

When I first met the man from Hot Springs,
  it was a hot and sultry day.
He was talking about war, so I listened close
  to all he had to say.
I could tell that he was very different
  from the others I had met before.
He seemed so noble, so brave, and courageous,
  who could ask for anything more?
The path he had us follow was not an easy one,
  and many were afraid to go down it.
But I followed him as far as I could,
  and of that, I've never regretted.
For they say that if you are courageous,
  that men will believe in you.
But if, with your courage, you have compassion,
  then men will follow you too.
And the day it came when he led the way,
  and I could not follow.
I had lost him in the tracts of time,
  and with that loss, felt sorrow.
Now time has passed, and yet I wonder,
  where do we get such men?
To make this world safe in times of peril,
  on his type we must depend.

I was talking to his daddy just the other day,
  and he said his grave ain't far.
Said he died trying to save another's life,
  and they gave him the Silver Star.
I thought how the people of Hot Springs
  must be very proud of him.
His country called, and Mike Thomas went,
  and he gave up his life for them.

And what I will always remember about Mike,
   is how he led the way.
Never asking his men to go, where he would not go,
   but always leading the way.

When I first met the man from Hot Springs,
   it was a hot and sultry day.
When I first met the man from Hot Springs,
   he was leading all the way.

His Old Commanding Officer

Kellan Kyllo
USMC, HMM-162, Ky Ha, Marble Mountain,
Quang Tri, Vietnam, 1966–1968

In air terminals
he always looked for him,
getting off a plane from the past.

John McCook
E-6, USA, Special Forces 5th Div,
Vietnam, 1964–1965

I was about seven when Ricky's family moved to our neighborhood. We lived at 2048 S. Haggert St. and they moved into 2047. Ricky and I took to one another immediately and soon became close friends. We both attended school at Visitation B.V.M. School about a mile or so from home. There were no buses then, so we walked together both ways, every day.

We were always ready to compete in just about anything and always wanted to be on the same team. We played baseball, football, basketball, hockey, and other sports. We found out that we had a lot in common in addition to our Irish heritage. We played with many friends in the neighborhood, but our relationship was special. Things went well for us early on, both at play and in school.

Eventually, we went on to the North Catholic High where we were on the football team together. We were treated well by the brothers there, who had a reputation for being strict. Finally came graduation day and we were so happy. We both agreed that it took a long time in coming.

It was not long after I found a job that I found out that my Dad was gravely ill with cancer. He lingered about a year before he died and I was devastated losing him. I thought my world had come to an end. Ricky and his family proved to be my family's greatest comfort.

The following year, 1963, June 17th I received my draft notice. I couldn't wait to find Ricky to see if he got his. He told me that he was going to join the Marines. I was not surprised because he always wanted to go one step more than anyone else.

Who knows what would have happened had he waited for his draft notice. He was serving a tour in Nam when he stepped on a land mine, killing him instantly. The news of his death was almost more than his family could bear. I knew I lost the best friend a guy could ever have and I went off by myself and cried. I remembered all the good times we shared. I will always remember Ricky for the good friend I had in him. Memorial Day and Veterans Day are very important to me for I am a vet and I remember my comrades. I never travel to Philadelphia that I don't stop at the Vietnam Veterans Memorial to say, "Hi" and "Nice to have known you, Ricky."

———

Clyde Q.
Corporal, USMC (R), South Korea, 1950–1951

I'll never forget my close friends who had their limbs blown off, screaming and crying as they were being evacuated from the front lines. They were young Marines that I had gone on liberty with in Osaka, Japan, while we waited to be embarked aboard an LST for the invasion of Inchon, South Korea.

When the enemy artillery projectiles began to explode around us, I was among them . . . and received only a concussion. Deep inside, I now feel guilty that it was my friends who died, and not me. Why was I left to live, when so many good men died?

In my dreams I recall the rugged terrain of the Taebeck Mountains in sub-zero cold, covered with snow and ice. I see two Marines, both wounded and trying to make their way to the casualty station. Each is supporting the other. As they struggle to stay on their feet, they are dragging a dead Marine behind them. The dead Marine is frozen stiff as a board.

That dream haunts me. Perhaps if I had been with them instead of where I was, maybe my additional firepower would have helped to make a difference.

He Wasn't Sure

Kellan Kyllo
USMC, HMM-162, Ky Ha, Marble Mountain,
Quang Tri, Vietnam, 1966–1968

He went to Washington, D.C.
to the Vietnam Veterans' Memorial
stared at the wall,
fell to the ground,
cried,
looked for his own name.

David A. Somerville
Sergeant, USA, 2/502 Inf Bn 101st Airborne Div Hq Co,
Camp Eagle, Vietnam, 1970–1971

He went to Vietnam and never came home
Far across the ocean, my spirit still roams
The days have slipped into many a year
And I have filled a river with sorrow's tears

Up in the attic, touching, and smelling his clothes
I have tried to go forward, but this book I can't close
And where do I take flowers to honor him?
There is no marked grave . . . Oh, the sin

The children are grown and all on their own
All I have left now are his memories and this empty home
In Washington . . . I sought out his name on the Wall
The memories rushed in, he was so handsome and tall

I have looked for an answer to explain all of this
Tired, I fall asleep dreaming of his last kiss
Thank God for allowing me these memories and more
In sweet dreams . . . He waits for me on heaven's shore

To the mothers, wives, family, and friends
Hold on to your dreams, for someday you'll see him again
Only God knows why this terrible thing has happened to us
But we must hold on, in God we must trust

I know it is hard to go on year after year
But the day is coming when he'll dry every tear
You'll see that father, son, and brother once more
His open arms will greet you, when you reach heaven's shore.

To a Marine Comrade

Charles Felix
Corporal, USMC, W.W. II:
Bougainville, Guam, Iwo Jima

Laughing, stalwart warrior,
Dead these many years.
It seems that only yesterday,
We shared our youthful dreams.
I recall you so very clearly,
That it seems you cannot be gone.
But on a tropic island

Your lonely cross bears silent testimony,
That God has called you home.

Author's note: Dedicated to a very close friend who enlisted with me,
and who died in the muddy Tenaru.

Ralph "Tripper" Sirianni
Sergeant, USMC, 2nd Bn 7th Reg,
Vietnam, 1969–1970

As an artist, I can no longer create work that's "happy." I'm much too aware of the pain and sadness in this world. That's what comes out on canvas . . . that's what's real.

Letters From Home

Michael Harac
Corporal, USMC, Vietnam

On my mother's side, I had no grandparents, no aunts, no uncles, and no cousins, all perished during the Holocaust. My mother was the only member of her family who emigrated from Poland to the United States She was consumed by guilt that she alone survived.

Years later I was to suddenly understand what her survival meant. In 1967, I returned to the United States after having served with the Marines in Vietnam. I considered myself lucky; I felt guilty about feeling lucky; I felt guilty that I killed; I felt guilty that I didn't do enough. I tried to understand the source of these feelings of guilt.

I tried to equate my guilt with that of my mother. My guilt was nothing compared to hers, how could it be? One could not understand the guilt she felt: you can never get rid of it, you can never take it away. You carry guilt with you; you can't relieve someone of that burden—it cannot be shared or delegated. It stays with you, and you learn, somehow, to live with it.

She would live with it alone: It was hers and hers alone, after all.

Grief and Loss

Thomas N. "Tommy" Bills
Sergeant, USA, 2/7th Cav (Gary Owen Bde) 1st Cav Div
Vietnam, 1965–1966

For so long I would not even think about the grief and loss. I was sure that if I just let go and "felt" it, I would never resurface from the pit! There was *so* much down there. I was totally fearful of what would happen if ever I decided to look . . . I was afraid I would find there was too much for me to handle.

Then I was fortunate enough to fall into the company of some men who were also suffering as I was. Together we took the plunge! I wasn't willing to leap right into the abyss. I reluctantly peered over the edge, then tentatively eased a leg over the side, then, holding tightly to the support of the other men in the group I finally lowered myself into the feelings. And to my great surprise, I was able to resurface and still go about my daily business! The grief and loss were there, and hit me hard at times, but with help I was able to cope with them.

Good news! It was a necessary process for me to leave the past behind. Having grieved the losses, I have resurfaced, and I'm still alive and breathing.

I Did Not Die

Central Highlands, Circa 1969

Do not stand at my grave and weep,
I am not there, I do not sleep.

I am a thousand winds that blow,
I am the softly falling snow.

I am the gentle showers of rain,
I am the fields of ripening grain.

I am in the morning hush,
I am in the graceful rush
Of beautiful birds in circling flight.
I am the starshine of the night.

I am in the flowers that bloom,
I am in a quiet room.
I am in the birds that sing,
I am in each lovely thing.

Do not stand at my grave and cry.
I am not there, I did not die.

Editors' note: Throughout the years, this poem has appeared in many places (including Jeffrey J. Clarke's *The Final Years: The U.S. Army in Vietnam*) and in many forms. Although authorship is usually believed to be unknown, it in fact was written in 1942 by Baltimorean Mary Frye. On the back of a brown paper bag Frye wrote the poem for a friend whose mother had died in Germany; the daughter had been unable to attend the funeral because of W. W. II.

6

ESCAPE

"What would the guys who died in Nam do if they got a
second chance to be alive, like me?
Don't ruin the life you got by surviving it."
Jack S.

The world can overpower the veteran's defenses at any stage of experiencing combat trauma. Drugs, alcohol, and attempts to psychologically "numb-out" the pain are common ways to shut out the nightmares and flashbacks.

Vets write of moving repeatedly across the country, constantly switching homes and jobs. Some try to escape their problems, leaving both problems and bad memories behind as they search for some place to start anew. Others chase acceptance, but often reject it unless it comes on their terms. For some, the workaday trials of a steady job, whether white- or blue-collar, seem trivial in light of the past accomplishments in combat. They disdain and minimize what they do for their paycheck, and seek fulfillment, a taste of the "life-and-death" intensity of the past when they were important and essential members of a team. It can be difficult to face life when a vet feels he peaked out at the age of 19.

Suicide is an enticing option to some, less frightening than continuing to run, to deteriorate, to despair, or to flame in anger at loved ones.

But the writings demonstrate that these veterans did not truly escape. Moreover, they turned, faced, and sought to overcome the pain and fear that drove them. Some see it as an obligation to those they left behind, others an obligation to their family, and others, to themselves—not to give up!

Today I Gave In

Dennis R. Tenety
Lance Corporal, USMC (Ret), 1st Marine Division
India Co 1st Plt 3rd Bn 5th Reg, An Hoa, Vietnam, 1969

I know I'll never be the same. My mind lives the memories day and night. When I reach out to hold someone I see only a grunt die in my arms. When I make love, the scenes of battle race through my mind. I have to push away. My body trembles no end. The pain is there, but I don't cry. I only grow colder. How I want so much to hold, caress, and enjoy life with someone. It will never be possible until I feel the pain. The hurt is there, but it is buried so deep. I've learned to accept loneliness. It is much easier to show rage than to feel emotions. My only pain is for my brothers slain in battle. They are the heroes. I can't feel the loss for anyone else, not even family. If I knew this would be the outcome, I would have let myself die that day. I am so lost being here. I know I can never give myself to anyone else.

There is a debt I owe my brothers who have fallen needlessly: it is on my dreams. It is in my mind. Everywhere I look I see those pitiful figures. Yet, as the days pass, I grow more tired. My will falters. But I remember my obligation to those nameless faces, and my will to live goes on. A false hero living off the blood of my brothers. My patience grows shorter as the days pass feeding the rage within me. There's so much going through my mind. I'm back to staying up for days. If I didn't turn to the drink and coke today, I would have fallen into the pill bottle. I'm sorry.

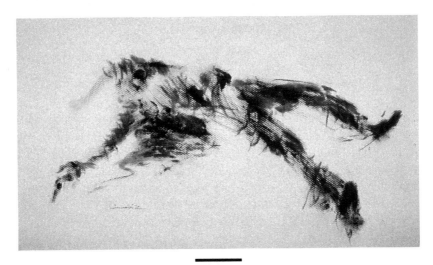

Suicide

Ralph "Tripper" Sirianni
Sergeant, USMC, 2nd Bn 7th Reg,
Vietnam, 1969–1970

"In memory of two fellow workers and Nam vets,
who committed suicide within two months of each other."

Craig Brandt
Specialist/4, USA, Army Security Service,
8th Radio Research Field Station,
Phu Bai, Vietnam, 1967–1968

After I was discharged from the army, I had a job as a counter clerk in a hi-fi repair shop for two years. I didn't make many new friends and I drank a lot, especially on weekends. But I would be sober by morning, and this made it easy for me to stay employed. I left that job and tried taking college courses. I did well in college but kept on drinking. I thought that if I got a job during the day and took more courses at night it would not leave me enough time or desire to drink, but I continued to drink and graduated from college with a degree in retail management. I then took a job with a retail chain. I could see that I was getting

nowhere there as my drinking continued and I was still alone. I made
lots of acquaintances but no new friends. So I quit that job and moved
to another state on the other side of the country. I got another job retail-
ing restaurant equipment, seemed to be getting my drinking under control, and was doing well socially. I met a nice girl, settled down, so I
thought. But then I was laid off, my wife was pregnant, and I started
drinking heavily again. My wife said I talked in my sleep and I would
awake out of breath and in a sweat.

I had five more jobs over the next seven years. But my wife, who
was a former nurse, got me to stop drinking and we moved to a new
town after our second child was born. Ten years later we were in a car
accident and my sleep disturbances have started again. Previously I
had not accepted any professional help, but now I am under the care of
a psychiatrist and find life to be a lot easier.

Drug Store

Rosemary A.
USA, Vietnam

The only real escape from existence; continuance of open-being
The only true feeling of reality, away from reality
It's a hard life to live—perhaps made so by yourself . . .
But an easy one to escape from, equally feasible.

There is no such thing as living free, natural, simple,
We are all slaves of an eternal master.
This is not a complete non-existence from this life, but yet
There are falsities for escape; patterns leading to pleasurable
    places where shelter is obtained if only for a moment.

A mysterious, colorful, lightning-riddled world set apart from a
    world of disgusting reality where pain, hate and
    deceit dwell . . .
Living under the protective guise of pleasure and happiness.
Always content with being alone, this world beckons to you
Assuring a never-involved state with the meaningless, repeating
    world which wastes the time of dead people.

Get away from the grind of reality, from human hurts that never
  cease.
Express yourself in fantasy, and forget yourself at face values.
Leave love alone, you are alone; it seems prophetic that such
  must be.
Yet, remain deliriously happy and content and live in your mysterious colorful, lightning-riddled world.

Jack S. P.A., R.N.
HM2, USN-USMC, 2nd Battalion 1st Marines,
1st Marine Division, Vietnam, 1968–1969

I guess I've been lucky in that I can't honestly say I've had PTSD.
Now, that's not to say I haven't felt and acted in a certain way. I still
wear my dogtags and see those days and think about them more than I
probably should. I even have a job similar to the one I had in Nam. I
work for the Medical Examiner investigating all kinds of terrible
deaths. One question has always kept me straight about the whole
thing: I've always asked myself what the guys who died in Nam would
do if they got a second chance to be alive like me. The answer is that
they would not be feeling bad or dredging up old memories. They
would be glad just to be alive as I was when I first came home. I say to
myself, sure you saw some bad things and did some bad things but
don't ruin the life you got by surviving it. Do it right for those who
didn't. We all owe them. The whole damn country does, so keep
straight for their memory; you didn't suffer any more than they did.

P.S. Maybe I haven't been so lucky.

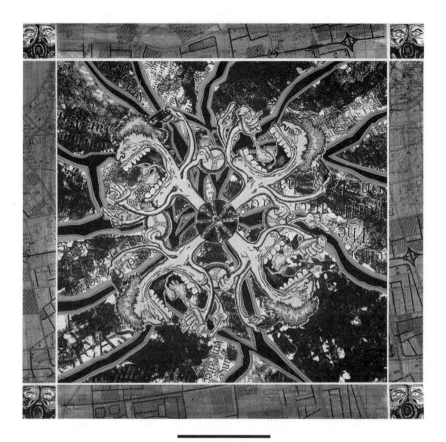

Bring to a Boil

Matt Doolin

Corpsman, Desert Storm

"Anger, and the many facets of PTSD."

To Find Himself

Kellan Kyllo
USMC, HMM-162, Ky Ha, Marble Mountain,
Quang Tri, Vietnam, 1966–1968

Road maps,
every state in the Union,
spread out
all over the floor.

No Big Deal

Walter "Angus" Vieira
Corporal, USMC, SLF 9th MAB RLT 26, 5th Marines,
Vietnam, 1967

Alone is how
I wanna live.
There's nothin' more
I wanna give.
To you or him
or her or me.
Just leave me
be.
Alone and free.
I can't keep
up.
With all your dreams.
That never end,
or so it seems.
I can't keep
livin!
Just your way.
Don't get upset
whenever I
say:
"I wanna be

alone.
You go your way."
My games,
not yours,
I wanna
play.
I'm not gonna
leave.
And you can
stay.
I just wanna
be
alone
today.
You go ahead.
I trust you
dear.
I just wanna
Stay alone. Right here. It's not who's
right
There ain't no
cause
for us to
fight.
You're just not
used
to me saying
no.
I just wanna
stay.
And you can go.

He Had Received a Medal
For
Saving Men's Lives
Kellan Kyllo
USMC, HMM-162, Ky Ha, Marble Mountain,
Quang Tri, Vietnam, 1966–1968

Didn't ever go anyplace,
lay
on the sofa in his basement,
looked at the ceiling,
drapes pulled dark,
quiet,
thought only of Vietnam.
The telephone rang again and again,
it rang a long time.

Dana S.
1st Lieutenant, USA Nurse Corps, Vietnam

I once saw a documentary called "The Boy in the Bubble." Born with total immunodeficiency, the boy was fated to once-removed contact with everything in the world. For a quarter of a century I also lived inside a bubble, which served similar protective functions. The bubble and its purposes evolved over time, but their origins lay in my return from Vietnam.

I arrived home with blood still under my fingernails; my last shift in pre-op had been both busy and long. My parents and siblings talked about the track team's prospects; I wondered if Khe Sanh would hold. I said the F-word during dinner; my mother blanched and my brothers sniggered. My family wondered when I would stop sleeping all day; I wondered when I would stop waking up looking for my boots and flak jacket. I also wondered how my replacement was doing—the one I, nonchalantly holding a severed arm, cordially welcomed into the OT. My parents worried about the blacks rioting in the streets; I worried about the blacks dying in the rice paddies.

My concerns were so alien to those of everyone around me! Everything moved too slowly back in the World; it was as if gravity had suddenly gained in force. I felt as if I had gotten on that home-bound freedom bird back in Vietnam only to land on the wrong planet. I didn't recognize my family, country, my society, myself. The friends I had been inseparable from before Vietnam now seemed frivolous and vacuous. I felt too old. People turned away from the look they saw in my eyes. People were either indifferent or hostile about Vietnam. I learned to seal my real feelings, along with my memories, inside the bubble. I tried to fit in. Fitting in succeeded only so long as I pretended to be just like everyone around me.

But I knew I had irrevocably changed. The "before" me was a naive, idealistic, eager girl; the "after" was altogether different, but bewilderingly elusive. The "before" me had been an energetic nurse; the "after," an overage actress who was always on-stage. I was out of step, out of tune, just plain "out of it"—whatever "it" was. I was different, defective, contaminated. My bubble enlarged and solidified.

I compartmentalized various aspects of my life inside the bubble. One compartment contained my grief and bewilderment over the loss of my youthful innocence and lightheartedness, the loss of my former self. Another contained unnerving yet tender memories of too many boys whose bodies and futures had been shattered. Yet another cell deep inside the bubble contained my secret, pervasive feelings of alienation and estrangement from everyone around me. What was left— what was not sealed off—was merely a facade. I looked like my former self, sounded like my former self, but I felt nothing. I had become an android. I was dead, but just didn't have enough sense to fall down.

Suicide was not an option; I had a son and would not inflict that horror on him. For years my feelings for him were the only feelings I had. But I secretly wanted only to be dead. Every day I had to renew my determination not to kill myself. The bubble kept me, and those around me, safe from my emotions.

As the years passed, my self-made bubble sealed Vietnam off even from me. Most of the time I didn't even remember that I had been there. I never thought of myself as a Vietnam veteran; only men were called veterans. I couldn't figure out what was wrong with me. Those heroic books about Florence Nightingale and Clara Barton that we girls grew up on never mentioned that Ms. Nightingale had spent the last 60 years of her life after the Crimean War in her bedroom, nor did they note that after the Civil War, Clara Barton had likewise spent years in a crippling depression. We women took care of everyone else; no notice was ever taken that we might need to be taken care of. No one ever warned me that I would pay a price for caring, nor that the cost of my caring would be so high.

In 1985 the bubble burst—"erupted" would perhaps be more descriptive—on the tenth anniversary of the fall of Saigon. Images of those last awful days were replayed nightly on television. Suddenly I could no longer deny that it had been real; yes, it had been as bad as, worse than, I had allowed myself to remember. I, together with several million male veterans, had been participants in a human tragedy of monumental proportions, and everyone else had, by their silence, their aversion, or their hostility, told me to make it go away for them. I was belatedly enraged: a bunch of rich white men had sent an army of teenagers halfway around the world so that their lives could be pissed away for nothing, and those arrogant old goats had never been held accountable. Instead, that army of teenagers, including me, were the ones who had been held accountable. The continuing suffering of the South Vietnamese who had believed in our government's promises was paralleled by the continuing suffering of our veterans who had believed those same words.

The weight of all that suffering was too much for me to bear. I could no longer carry it around in my bubble as a sacrifice on behalf of those for whom it was more convenient not to be bothered by the war. I collapsed under the weight of it all. I was engulfed by the enormity of the suffering that I had both witnessed and endured. I couldn't eat; I couldn't sleep; I couldn't be "nice" anymore. I could no longer be the "good girl" I was raised to be, the ideal woman who put up and shut up. I was one more pissed off Viet vet. At the same time I couldn't figure out what had happened. Why is this bothering me now? Why did I wait so long to give up trying to fit in and instead let out a good, healthy "No!"?

I'll never put up and shut up again. I will no longer do what society expects its women to do: clean up after all the shit others make without comment or complaint, all for a pat on the head and the privilege of living in some man's shadow. I am no longer a nice lady who wants only to help. I'm a Vietnam veteran with a badass attitude. I'm still fighting a war. I'm almost 50 years old, and I've been in treatment for PTSD for seven years. My husband wants to know when it will be over. Well, my war will never be over. Until the last aged Vietnam veteran dies, a footnote in some Wednesday night newscast, this miserable, filthy war will never be over.

7

FAMILY AND OTHER PERSPECTIVES

"We're amazed at all the courage you demonstrate each day.
We love you, Dad!"
Mary, Michelle, and Danny

"My relationship with my husband became one of
a caretaker . . . I hope attention will be given to
family members so they can support their loved one—but
not at the expense of themselves."
Kay, ex-wife of a veteran

Combat trauma affects not only the veteran, but his or her family and community as well.

Partners, parents, siblings, and friends report the veteran returns from war a different person. The veteran knows that he or she has changed and feels isolated by the sense of being different, never the same again. Some veterans cannot find the words to share their combat experiences with spouses who want nothing more than to understand and help their husband or wife. In anger, and in sadness, the vet demands, "How can anyone who hasn't been there understand?" The spouses of other vets refuse to listen, not wanting to hear about their husband's or wife's life or "adventures" before marriage, frightened by what they might learn. Friends and family alike adopt the view of "It's over—put it behind you." Regardless of who it is that raises barriers against communication, the vet is driven further into isolation exactly at the time he or she is in greatest need of support.

Family members and friends share the veteran's isolation, and the depth of emotion in family writings reflects the importance of support to the veteran and to the family surviving combat trauma. Some see their veteran spouse or parent in an almost heroic light, marveling at their courage in spite of the burdens their veteran carries. Vets often find their reason for living in an understanding spouse and children.

Yet, there are limits to all things. Not understanding his or her behavior, but wanting to help their loved one live a more balanced life, family members can grow impatient. They make demands for change that the vet may be incapable of meeting. Spouses will frequently take increasing responsibility for the veteran and the rest of the family, a burden which can develop into resentment and lead to divorce. Veterans mourn the loss of their spouse and children, and damn themselves for pushing their loved ones away.

Families of POWs and MIAs have an important part of their lives suspended in the past. Having no confirmed loss of their loved one, they wonder each day if the veteran is alive and clutch at hope for his return.

Would You Dare to Care?

Jane Seawell
Wife of Vietnam Veteran Stephen Seawell, Sp/5
USA, Combat Medic, 4th Inf Div 2/35th Inf, 1968–1969

The righteous in his padded pew
Gave greetings home:
"We don't know you . . .
We can't comprehend
You are distressed
While we feel blessed
To be so much alive."
On this, their conscience thrives.

Who shares the agony
Of sights and sounds we'll never see?
"Forget it all," the righteous say,
"It's in the past, all put away."
Their smugness deeper hurts and scars
The man who gave his youth for ours.
"Don't rock the boat!
With guilt we won't tote
For men who bled and died.
Don't make us think.
Forget the past.
Be thankful you're alive.
We're happy, free, and busy we'll stay.
Vietnam veteran—don't get in our way!
The world we live in is secure,
Your cries for help we can't endure."

But wait! Who carries that Vietnam vet
Who, in his mind's eye still sees
The brave comrades who suffered and died
So we can all be free?
Who really cares to give a hand
To the veteran lost in his own land?

"God set him free!"
That is my plea,
From a war that continues to slay.

Who dares to care? I dare to care!
As I live with my Vietnam vet.
I've counted the cost,
For much I have lost,
The world would say I'm in debt.

But God is my guide,
In Him will I hide,
For that is the place of sweet rest.
And on that glad day,
When we meet, God will say:
"A crown I now give,
To my servant who lived
With a war-torn Vietnam vet."

Dedicated to every veteran of the Vietnam War. I personally thank you
for the freedom I still enjoy. May God bless you and set you free from
the sins of this nation.

PTSD: A Family Perspective

Kay
Ex-Wife of a Veteran

As the wife of a Vietnam veteran who is 100 percent disabled due to
PTSD, I don't know where to begin describing the effects that my husband's condition has had on our family. Initially diagnosed as having
bi-polar disorder after years of drug and alcohol abuse, he was treated
with lithium, which helped alleviate some of his symptoms for a short
period of time. The problems (rage, depression, social and emotional
withdrawal, insomnia, and so on) soon returned and upon re-evalua-
tion, his diagnosis was changed to PTSD. Before this time, I thought

that my husband dealt with his experiences in Vietnam very well. I believed this despite the fact that he avoided discussing the war at all costs, had been emotionally distant ever since I met him, and had never maintained a job for any length of time.

After his diagnosis, I spent a great deal of time researching PTSD and talking with counselors at the VA so that I would have some knowledge of what we were dealing with. I felt very optimistic regarding our future and his prognosis, as I felt that we could overcome anything as long as we worked together. Plus, "R" had finally allowed me to get closer to him emotionally, and I considered this a big step.

Following out-patient therapy, "R" began going into the hospital for intensive in-patient therapy for periods of six weeks and more every few months, and this, plus the effects of the prescribed medication, increasingly interfered with his job. Although his symptoms had gotten progressively worse, the job gave him something to look forward to each day. In fact, work seemed to be the only thing he was interested in, as he increasingly withdrew from our two children and me. He rarely had anything to say to us and was usually asleep. Upon waking up, he would eat, take a bath, then go to bed. Any attempt to draw him into conversation or to get him to go anywhere or do anything with us was met with anger, so we all learned to leave him alone. This became a pattern, and the children and I got used to him being home physically but not emotionally.

In the meantime, our children began having their own problems due to "R's" illness. Our oldest began seeing the guidance counselor at school, as well as another counselor, because she did not understand what was happening to her Daddy. The frequent hospitalizations caused both children to feel abandoned. They were confused because their Daddy "looked fine—so why was he in the hospital?" Behavioral problems required further work with each child. When home, my husband virtually turned the role of disciplinarian over to me—probably due to guilt over his absences—but the children quickly learned that they could play the two of us against each other to their benefit.

Another major problem was that we became isolated from our friends and neighbors. "R" was often asleep when we got home, so the children had to be quiet and not wake him. This prevented them from having their friends over to play, and this isolation soon spread to all areas of our lives. I could never be sure what kind of mood "R" would be in, so I discouraged people from coming to our home. This problem was exacerbated because he went into a rage when a few friends of the children were here. Naturally, the parents did not want their children to come here anymore, which further hurt our girls.

Eventually, "R" quit his job and applied for 100 percent disability due to PTSD. My relationship with my husband became one of caretaker, which was my fault. I believed that by taking care of him I could make him better. I assumed all responsibilities in our household: paying bills, house maintenance, buying groceries, cooking, child care, helping with homework, cutting the grass, and on and on. I truly believed that by removing all responsibility from my husband, he would be able to concentrate on his problems and get better. Unfortunately, this is not what happened. I only hope that in the future more attention will be given to family members so they can support their loved one— but not at the expense of themselves.

<hr>

Cheryl P. Burrows
Wife of Vietnam Veteran

Twenty-seven years ago
Yet, it feels like you were there yesterday.
Rainy days, helicopter sounds, Chinese food, war movies,
    fireworks,
parades, digging in the dirt, humidity, crying children, and death.
Who knows what else brings back your memories?
It's a great, gaping, bleeding hole.
We tried to ignore it, but it snuck up and captured us.

A Real Hero

Cynthia S.
USMC Wife

A real Hero
has courage
to fight
for anything
except himself.

Real Heroes believe always in
their hearts
they are Heroes
at the moment.

Real Heroes
later discover
and invent
consequences and regret
for what
they achieved.

Real Heroes
never realize
that sometimes
life offers
no choices
especially
when taught
not to choose.

Real Heroes
continue
to fight
and conquer
daily
with courage
unrecognized
by their hearts.

Real Heroes
someday
will discover
they already control
all of
the courage
they will ever need
not to remain
a Real Hero
and simply
be themselves.

The VA

Cheryl P. Burrows
Wife of Vietnam Veteran

Therapy. Drugs. Support groups. Hospitalizations.
Blame, pain, can't cope, and shame.
PTSD. Depression. Skin rashes. Is there Agent Orange, too?
What is the cure? Do they even know?
The VA.

Peggy Crowder
Sandy Crowder
CWO III, USA, W.W. II, Korea,
Vietnam (2nd Bn 60th Inf 9th Inf Div)

Many men were suffering from stress after Vietnam, but none of them
knew what was wrong. At age 43, my husband was no spring chicken
when he was sent to Vietnam, with W.W. II and Korea behind him. He
went because it was his job. He wrote me about what was happening in
Vietnam to the men he served with and himself. I was shocked when I
met him in Hawaii. I didn't even recognize him because of the weight
he had lost and how sick he was from hepatitis. He was too sick to do

anything the two weeks we had together. The tears every night were unbearable. I had to force him to get on the stupid bus for the plane ride back to Vietnam.

He made it home in October 1969. No bands, no welcome except from family. We lived near a highway and every time a truck would pass, he dove for cover. We bought the new truck he wanted, but I was shocked to find he didn't remember buying it. Nor did he remember his brother and sister visiting. Rather than return to Vietnam for another full tour of duty, he retired with 25 years of service.

He wanted to mount guns on each corner of the small house we bought in Indiana, just to be prepared. This was not my husband! My husband was a quiet man who seldom lost his temper. He didn't like the way America was treating the Vietnam veteran.

The people never mentioned PTSD at the VA hospital when he went there for Chloracne, which they diagnosed as sun poisoning. After numerous heart attacks and a triple bypass, my husband suffered kidney failure, needing dialysis three times a week. The VA hospital was no help. After the way the VA treated him, he swore he'd never go back. And I promised him he would not have to, as long as I could make it without VA help.

Because the VA had no record of his volunteering for mustard gas testing in 1944, nor did they have his Vietnam records, he was denied a service connection for his medical problems. When you see yourself facing bankruptcy with a husband so sick even the doctors don't give him much hope and you ask the VA at least to give him his medicines and they refuse this veteran of 25 years, that's stress.

My family doctor sent me to the local military hospital for the rash I developed on my legs after sorting the clothes my husband brought back from Vietnam. The military doctor laughed and told me it was a classic case of Chloracne. He gave me the same medicine used to treat soldiers returning from Vietnam. A week after taking the medicine, my muscles were so weak, I couldn't raise my arms over my head. Then I couldn't keep my eyes open.

I saw 13 doctors in a two-year period and was told my problems were "all in your head." Sometimes when I couldn't make my legs and eyes do what I wanted, I did question my own sanity. Finally (many more doctors and several wrong diagnoses later) a research program told me I have something similar to Myasthenia Gravis. In 1991, an Air Force doctor told me I definitely had been contaminated by Agent Orange, but I would never see any money for it. Now I have loss of feeling in my legs due to poor circulation, and the VA won't help me because I'm not a veteran.

If I was a veteran, I'd be entitled to benefits, but because I'm a civilian I do not count. Well, I do count! I never volunteered to be contaminated by our own government. They have tested some of the men, few of the babies, none of the wives.

I was 37 when this first happened to me. I am now 61, still fighting with a government that does not give a damn.

Stress? You bet!

That's When He Started Drinking

Kellan Kyllo
USMC, HMM-162, Ky Ha, Marble Mountain,
Quang Tri, Vietnam, 1966–1968

His wife
couldn't listen any longer,
or read
what he had written about it,
or even think
about that side of her husband.
So she bitched at him all the time instead.

Cynthia S.
USMC Wife

I'm the third wife of a Vietnam veteran with PTSD. We've been married for 14 years. At 18, I met my husband and was fascinated with him. He seemed so manly, so rugged but very gentle. I was proud of him for being in Vietnam.

He was silent often, but when we talked, it was for hours. He seemed sad about the war and his previous marriages. I didn't realize he had PTSD, as he kept everything inside. I felt sorry for him, thinking he needed me. I thought I could make him feel better by making the difference in his life.

Early in our marriage, I tried to control his actions by giving him ultimatums or conditions for me to stay. Now because of the PTSD and his physical problems, I have to control many things, which I really don't want to do any longer. Every time my husband hurt me, I would hurt him back and it became more and more difficult to get any reaction from him. I've learned from therapy and the VA women's groups that my attempts to control him or retaliate just made things worse for me, for him, and for our 14-year-old son. I was inflicting most of the pain upon myself.

I was driving myself crazy trying to transform my husband into what I wanted him to be. I daydreamed about how romantic, sensitive, and compassionate our lives would be if only he'd change. After many painful years, I no longer try to change him, but to change myself. He will never be what I want. I have to accept him the way he is.

For me, living with my husband has been a revelation because I have learned so much about myself; and I'm still learning. I know I'm not responsible for his actions. I don't know if our marriage will last because I keep growing and learning and he does not, but I don't worry about it. I know I can rely on myself. It's a sad situation and it would be so easy to feel sorry for both of us, but I cannot. I enjoy life too much. I look forward to getting out of bed every day, doing things for myself. PTSD is like cancer, only worse because it spreads to those you love. Even though my husband lives in Vietnam in his mind, when he comes home for vacations I am there waiting for him, just one day at a time.

Aftermath of Killing

Kellan Kyllo
USMC, HMM-162, Ky Ha, Marble Mountain,
Quang Tri, Vietnam, 1966-1969

Enemy bodies of tossed and twisted
arms
and legs,
with eyes dried open
that could no longer see,
or blink,
hidden
in the quiet of a person
over a prolonged period of time,
exposed themselves
when
he and his wife made love.

To the Lady of My Life

Dennis R. Tenety
Lance Corporal, USMC (Ret), 1st Marine Division
India Co 1st Plt 3rd Bn 5th Reg, An Hoa, Vietnam, 1969

Here I am, soaring in my glory, because I have you. You have turned my life around. For once I can look forward to the future, although at one time the future had no meaning for me. My world was coming to a dead end.

There was a time I thought our lives would never be able to come together. It seemed the odds were stacked against me.

For once I have a reason to be happy for beating the odds. It is a first for me to feel this way. I have never experienced a love so strong, kind, generous, and understanding as yours. You are one in a million, and I won the grand prize!

Babe, thank you for giving me a reason to look forward to the tomorrows that will come, for I know my tomorrows will be spent loving you.

Ken Sauvage
Corporal, USMC, 2nd Bn 3rd Marines,
Vietnam, 1968–1969

I married late, after I had some grip on my own life. I am lucky to have a wife who makes an effort to understand my attempts to cope with the emotions and memories. She understands how I have been created, in part, by those experiences. She has her own ghosts and one of the bases of our relationship is mutual support.

Duane A. "Tubby" Brudvig
Specialist/5, USA, Vietnam, 1969–1970

Family members should have been informed that we were going to be very different people from the ones who left to go to war. We were very wary of our surroundings, jumpy, nervous, quick to deal with danger physically, and had to be awakened very carefully. We had been conditioned for rocket attacks, taking fire, killing without wasting time.

Families should have been informed that Vietnam veterans are subject to strange moods and drug and alcohol abuse, which affect the whole family.

Even when my daughters were little, it bothered them. My youngest wrote a small poem in school about it that tore me up inside. My oldest daughter has tried to understand it the best she can. My wife just didn't want to see me suffer anymore. They all suffered right along with me in their own way. Vietnam was almost 24 years ago, but it is something we as a family have to deal with day by day. I would like families to know that we want to be normal again and that it will take time and a lot of counseling, but it is getting better!

Ralph "Tripper" Sirianni
Sergeant, USMC, 2nd Bn 7th Reg,
Vietnam, 1969–1970

My immediate family (parents, siblings, wife, and children) must have felt as though I was a stick of dynamite. Sometimes I'd go off . . . or else the fuse would die and they'd wait, wondering when I'd explode again. Family members can become aware of the triggers that light the fuse. Those who live with an individual who suffers from combat trauma can learn to take precautions to avert "unhealthy situations." These precautions vary with different individuals.

Michelle Sirianni
Wife of Vietnam Veteran

I coped by praying a lot, and I became educated about PTSD. Family members need patience, understanding, and communication.

For My Family—Who Don't Understand Me

Dennis R. Tenety
Lance Corporal, USMC (Ret), 1st Marine Division
India Co 1st Plt 3rd Bn 5th Reg, An Hoa, Vietnam, 1969

I've been home over two decades, but there is no need for *me* to keep track. The few times I see you, you remind me: "Find a direction. Set your goals in life. You should find God. Cut your hair. Shave that beard. Stop living in the past. Leave the war behind you. It's over 20 years since you've been home from Vietnam."

These words are easy for anyone to say, especially when they did not fight the war in Vietnam. I realize your failure to understand was partly my fault. The letters I wrote always said, "The weather's nice. Having a good time. Don't worry. It's safe where I am, no fighting here. Be home soon." It was all lies. I didn't want anyone to worry.

I should have written the truth. Chances are you might have understood. I never wrote about the fear racking my mind and body, or my first day landing in a hot L.Z., with many more to follow. Never did I write how many times I thought I was going home in a coffin. Never did my letters tell the odds stacked against my life: chances were I'd be wounded or killed the first month. Life expectancy in a fire fight was six seconds.

Would you then have understood?

Frank-Josip Racic
Sergeant, USA, Vietnam, 1968–1970

PTSD has far-reaching ramifications for myself and my family. Recently my thirteen-year-old son was hospitalized for two weeks with chronic acute depression.

Animals Are Better Than People

Kellan Kyllo
USMC, HMM-162, Ky Ha, Marble Mountain,
Quang Tri, Vietnam, 1966–1968

His dog
looked at him with eyes
of love,
when
the whole country did not.

Ken Sauvage
Corporal, USMC, 2nd Bn 3rd Marines,
Vietnam, 1968-1969

I have been honest with my children. I answer their questions and, within reason, explain my feelings and behavior. I have taken them to the Wall and cried in front of them. Without trying to indoctrinate, I want them to understand the long-term impact of war on human beings. I feel that we, the children of World War II veterans, did not receive any sense of the reality of their war from either our parents or our culture.

Dennis R. Tenety
Lance Corporal, USMC (RET), 1st Marine Division
India Co 1st 3rd Bn 5th Reg, An Hoa, Vietnam, 1969

Your only debt to me is an answer for my children. Why did they have to see me at my worst? Then tell me about your compensation.

God Knows We Need You

Children of Michael Rice
RM-2, USN, PBR River Boats,
Dong Ha River Security Group,
Cua Viet River, Vietnam, 1968-1969

For Father's Day 1992

We're amazed at all the courage you demonstrate each day.
The way you smile through sorrow and shrug the tears away.
We know your heart is hurting, your eyes are filled with pain.
No matter where you run, heartache and fear remain.
But you just keep on smiling and telling us you're fine.
And we just keep on praying and asking God for time.

We know, deep inside our hearts, that God will grant us peace.
That He's the reason that you shine and how you stay at ease.
For He, in all His wisdom, has looked upon your face.
And given you this strength, because you're needed in this place.

We love you, Dad!
Mary, Michelle, and Danny

An Open Letter To My Children

Dennis R. Tenety
Lance Corporal, USMC (Ret), 1st Marine Division
India Co 1st Plt 3rd Bn 5th Reg, An Hoa, Vietnam, 1969

I told you the importance of respect and feelings; that if you are honest you will never have to be afraid. I showed you how much it means to have people you care for—to have their trust and friendship. I taught you the value of treating someone the way you would like to be treated; of never judging people for their appearance or beliefs. If you don't agree with them you can always walk away.

I know these values. I had to learn them the hard way, as did many of my friends in Vietnam. A place not many of my friends came home from. I never wanted you to live or learn the way we did.

I am sorry though, that when I tried to teach you about love it all came apart. I realize now that I can't teach you something I don't understand. I have failed at that all these years. When I should have been learning about love, they were preparing my life for a different chapter. I am truly sorry for the way things happened.

Do one thing as I do: respect your mother for what she did.

Take care of yourselves for me.

Love,
Your Dad

Now I Understand, Daddy

Sgt. Richard G. Lawrence
Combat Vietnam Veteran, USMC

"This picture never happened. I would like to hold my daughter,
before it's too late."

Backfire

Mary Moran
Vietnam Veteran, Sister of Vietnam Veteran

Discharge. A word loaded as an automatic weapon
with force of recoil and mechanical spring action
for repeatedly ejecting the empty cartridge shell,
introducing a new cartridge, and firing it.

John Fitzgerald Kennedy shot.
Martin Luther King, Jr. shot.

The assassination of his dreams
reeks of gun smoke and funeral flowers.

Honorable discharge from military duty at twenty,
thrown into a civilian stockade of antiwar sentiment:
How many babies did you kill? How many women did you . . . ?
Hey "brother," bring back any Cong skulls? Or good dope?

> Hot, humid daze. Saigon airport.
> Loading body bag after body bag.
> Some closed, some open. Eyes, mouths.
> He carried the weight of death home.

Discharge from involuntary commitment at mental hospitals.
Conditional release into court appointed conservatorship.
The guardian, keeper of his accounts and disability checks,
decides where and how he lives, now that he's free.

> Thorazine . . . mellaril . . . haldol . . .
> Magic bullets explode on impact.
> Shrapnel lodged in brain tissue
> shreds his thoughts, feelings, spirit.

Last definition. An act of relieving something or someone
that oppresses or is oppressed. Here lies the truth.
Discharge. I hear the word explode in our faces.
He's dead, and now a slug of lead festers in my heart.

> The final bullet fired
> targets this matter of choice.
> Grieving, we bury his bones
> and ask you for accountability.

The Cure?

Cheryl P. Burrows
Wife of Vietnam veteran

Pills and more pills.
Therapy. Try a new treatment. Read another book.
Talk, talk, and more talk.
What do you want?
Love, inner peace, hope, and happiness.
Is that too much to ask?
Is this the best it gets or the worst?
Throw me a lifeline.

Bittersweet

Sheral A. Clary (Thomas)

Thoughts of you today are . . . "Bittersweet" . . . For you see . . .
I am free . . .
Free to enjoy the company of some very colorful people . . .
Gypsies . . . Nomads if you will.
Free to work or not . . . Party or not . . . Love or not . . .
    the choice is mine.
I stand with a cold beer in my hand, among strangers,
    yet friends . .
Reminiscing back over the years . . . and we always keep coming
    back to you . . . .
Where you are . . . what you are doing . . . how you must
    be feeling . . .
The suffering, hopelessness, anger, and confusion you must
    endure.

God knows we miss you and still hope.
Some things are the way you remember . . .
Flowers still bloom in the spring . . .
Children still laugh and play . . .
The waters of the lake still glisten with silver . . .

Grass still has that fresh, newly-mown smell . . .
Clouds still build up into thunderstorms that you lay awake in
     the dark of night and listen to . . .
The sun and wind still feel like friends upon my face, as I ride on
     the back of a Harley across our land . . . Free.

It's sad to think . . . that not everyone has you on their minds,
all day and into the night . . . as I often do.
Sure . . . lots of things have changed . . .
But not the things that really matter . . . Freedom, Nature,
     Friends.

After the party was over I closed my eyes and shed a tear . . .
for all you are missing and all you have lost . . . So . . .
My thoughts are Bittersweet . . .
Bitter . . . for your loss of freedom . . .
Sweet . . . for all of the memories we have.

Author's note: 3/14/92 For Our POW/MIAs

To the Veterans I Know

Gloria J. Berman, LICSW
Group Therapist

A generation of young led on by thoughts of
     glory—dreams of manhood.
Vilified by fools who did not know enough
     to despise the war instead of the warriors.
Noble/ignoble deeds done by the frightened,
     valiant boys in their rite of passage.
Made to pay the price forever with scars that
     are indelible but do not show.

A generation of throw-away young—used, of no
     value.

Their innocence ripped away with startling
    brutality.
Knowing death with an intimacy greater than
    anything they have ever known—save fear.
You wanted no knowledge of what you had
    wrought.

You do not know what you have lost.
What you have held back, they have given to each
    other;
The glad embrace;
The proud smile;
The brotherhood.
Because you have held back, I take the right
    away from you.
You are undeserving and they are no longer
    boys.
Welcome home, Men.

———————

Laura A. Harris
Associate Member VVA Chapter 151, Bayonne, NJ

July 8, 1985

Dearest John:

They found 26 M.I.A.s today.

It was a lifetime ago when we shared our hope and dreams. I missed you every moment, every sunrise, every sunset. In the warm days of summer and the cold winter nights; your gentle touch has warmed my heart these many years that you have been gone.

My life has been caught between yesterday and tomorrow. My prayer was to be with you. You have always been with me. Never have you left my side. Your presence is strong. I know you are here with me now. I wish I could reach out and touch you, to hold you close, one last time.

Twenty-odd years have past, the long hours of waiting, the endless nights, the lonely years. Now the time has come for you to come home. I hope I am strong enough to greet you.

They found 26 M.I.A.s today.

Love always,

Laura

Deceit

Ralph "Tripper" Sirianni
Sergeant, USMC, 2nd Bn 7th Reg, Vietnam, 1969-1970

"All who suffer from PTSD are haunted by the guys we left behind."

A Letter to You 24 Years Later

Sheral A. Clary (Thomas)

Dear Any POW/MIA,

It doesn't seem possible that years have slipped away since I started my first letter addressed to: "Any Soldier."

Here I am, washing dishes after dark . . . my headphones on. Know what? I don't need the old songs to take me back to the memories of yesteryear. I wear them . . . in my heart.

Two names are still upon my wrist: Avery, 4-6-72 and Thomas, 7-6-71. Never could the letters that were sent to you, John Ware, Don Wilson, Larry Patrick, Ron Herrman, and the rest of "my guys"—be counted. And the Care Packages! It makes me smile, to remember. Do you remember? The scented envelopes with lipstick kisses. The kind words and pictures, and all of those cookies. The stories and the jokes we shared, and the bottles of after-shave and bars of soap. All of our dreams and hopes and prayers. Even though I only have your letters to reread over and over again, something tells me that you do remember. I may not know where you are, but my heart still cries, for those who are never forgotten.

Bring you home? Darlin', if only I could, you would be cherished, and treasured—as your memory is and like only "your girl" could do.

Wherever you are tonight, I just wanted you to know that you are not alone; you never were. I have always been there, right in your heart and your tears and in your pain. Am I sparking your memory? Yeah . . . The silly blonde-haired, blue-eyed girl that cared so very, very much for you so many tears and days ago. She still does, still hoping and praying that you will be home soon.

I miss you and I won't forget. Ever. I can't. I've loved you for a very long time.

Goodnight, my warrior. You are the best!

"Your girl" from the past.

Sleep Restless, My Love

Barry Powlas
Husband of Ann Powlas, Vietnam Nurse

I listen to your every breath,
Waiting for your first labored sigh,
Knowing it means the anguished pursuit
Of your subconscious by the never-ending
Nightmare of Vietnam.

Again the helpless anger surges in me,
But I know in my heart I cannot
Chase the demons that pursue you
From your mind.

I can only wake you, hold you, and tell you
"I love you and it will be all right," when
We both know that it is not, because the
Demons will return again another time.

But for now,
Just know I am here for you when you
Sleep restless, my love.

8

MAKING SENSE OF IT ALL

"I do not trust the world system, nor do I believe in the goodness of man. I accept the money from the VA for my disability as what I am due."
Robert di G.

"What therapy can do is make the past bearable by enabling me to formulate some meaning from the experience . . . I try to tell myself that I must be a good person . . . Would a bad person feel this much pain for this long?"
Dana S.

It is tempting to give the final chapter of *Soldier's Heart* an uplifting title, such as "Healing" or "Acceptance." These words are familiar to veterans. They're what vets seek and, indeed, write about, and would indicate a clear-cut, happy ending to their painful journey. "Integration" is a title that would be more familiar to treatment professionals than to veterans, but it is a tempting choice as well. In clinical terms, integration is finding meaning in the experience of traumatic events, growing as a person either because of, or in spite of, the traumatic experience, and ultimately developing a sense of spirituality—a bond—with the surrounding world.

Unfortunately, "surviving" combat trauma is not so simply defined and it would be less than accurate to use any of these words.

The subtitle to this book is *Survivors' Views of Combat Trauma*, yet none of the contributors write of "surviving combat trauma," or of "being healed" from it, as if PTSD, battle fatigue, or nervous disability were a distant wound, a thing of the past. They write of surviving combat, not its aftermath, of beginning to be healed, of doing things that help them to heal, or of healing as the goal to which they aspire. The veteran member of this book's editorial staff, after years of successful therapy in the Vet Center program, does not view himself as "healed," but as "healing" and has only recently accepted that he "survived" anything. Some veterans write of "acceptance," but they are very specific about what they have come to accept. Some write of accepting who they are; others of accepting the death of friends, but to these, healing still seems a goal.

If veterans do not write of becoming healed, and limit acceptance to this thing, or that, how do the writings in this chapter distinguish themselves from awareness of symptoms, despair, and grief?

The poetry and essays in this chapter are instilled with a sense of retrospection. Unlike prior chapters, there is a feeling of trying to *make sense of it all* that goes well beyond the raw cries of pain or the plea for help. Many veterans recount their traumatic and treatment experiences as they explain what they have come to accept and how they are being healed. In doing so, they show that healing, like living, is a process that involves passing through stages of growth and change as the veteran learns to reconnect to the world and regain control of his and her life.

The process of healing can be viewed as a series of plateaus, upon which veterans pause as they *make sense of their lives*. At each plateau, they can stop and live awhile—a lifetime if they choose—deciding to accept who and what they are. Or they can decide to go on, pursuing a greater sense of well-being within themselves or with society. In either case, vets demonstrate a growing skill at *taking control* of their lives by making choices. After years of responding to emotional triggers and depending on therapy or drugs, the ability to make choices is energizing.

Some veterans accommodate their lives to their trauma, even though they feel they will neither forgive nor forget what has happened to them. These vets seem angry to others, and they are. They may express an attitude of "this is as good as it gets," and they function in life and in society in spite of what has happened to them. These vets are surviving combat trauma and *they are healing*. They have a defined relationship with the world that serves their needs, and they can always reserve the right to change the relationship later.

Healing may begin as a string of "nots"—not having nightmares, not having flashbacks, not being angry all the time, not using drugs or alcohol, not abusing themselves or others, not being depressed. To veterans, or their families, who have lived decades with night horrors and erupting anger "not" doing these things anymore spells relief, and *they are healing*.

Hopefully, "making sense of it all" eventually leads to accepting the past, not reliving it. Acceptance requires remembering traumatic events, often in a therapeutic setting, and getting back in touch with the feelings connected to those events. It can mean accepting that you lived when others died, without having to forgive yourself for living. It can mean accepting the death of others, and honoring their memory without forever carrying the debilitating grief of their loss, or the hopeless burden of keeping them alive through thoughts. In accepting the past, the veteran looks at his or her present relationship with the world and begins to find happiness in it, *and the process of healing continues*.

The writings of veterans who appear to have integrated their traumatic experience into their lives differ significantly from those in earlier stages of dealing with their pain. They're reflective of the trials they've survived. They remember, but no longer relive the past, and are invested in the present, writing of choices, of being in control, and of feeling. They are hopeful for the future. Their stories feel considered and complete, absent of the immediacy of pain, as they put into words the meaning found in the traumatic experience so pivotal to their personal history. As they continue to reconnect within themselves and to their families, to make sense of their lives, *they continue to heal*. They begin to see that the person they once were is the person that they are. Made stronger and fuller by their traumatic experience they are able to participate in the activities of work, play, and love they once feared lost.

Thomas N. "Tommy" Bills
Sergeant, USA, 2/7th Cav (Gary Owen Bde) 1st Cav Div,
Vietnam, 1965–1966

It wasn't until I was around 44 years old
that a psychologist
   viewing my artwork
   spotted it.

I could look back and remember
how I had to stop doing a painting
   because something was wrong
   something didn't feel right.

When I was sculpting I'd have to stop
or change the sculpting in some way
   to change what I was beginning
   to see.

The psychologist pointed out
that something would emerge
   that would trigger an emotion
   or a memory
   of something from the past.

Whether through color or texture
   or smell or taste
I would recall
   something uncomfortable
   and want to be away from it.

With help from the doctor
   and the men's group
I began to let these paintings and sculptings
   emerge natural and uninhibited.

And I saw Vietnam again.

And I began to see childhood traumas.

And I began to heal from them!

The psychologist told me to paint about it
since I was having trouble talking about it.

It works!

I can let down my guard
not just from the imagined enemy today
    but from the crowd of past experiences.

Letting down my guard frees me to really feel
what happened to me as a child
and what is happening to me as a man
and with this freedom
    comes the ability to laugh
    and be me
    naturally.

It's important for me to laugh
    at what I was
    at what I've become
and to be loose and free about
    what I want to be!

To let go of the fears
    and all that holds me back
    from really being
    all that I can be.

When I become rigid in my painting
I loose my spontaneity
    and my "God flow"
    that lets me
    let God
    work through me.

If I can be playful and happy
in not just my art
   but in my work
   and my relationships

I truly am
   playful and happy.

If I'm inflexible
   everything seems hard to do
   and I'm unhappy.

So I'll continue to splash paint
   and hammer and chisel
   with abandon and enthusiasm
and be happy!

Remember

Joseph L. Findley
MR-E3, USN, Vietnam and Cambodia, 1970

Remember the faces and places,
Not the names and games,
Remember each sunrise,
But no sunset,
Remember what you can,
For some you cannot forget!

7-21-88 "Gypsy"

My name is Joseph L. Findley. I'm on my fourth Harley in 31 years riding experience. I was in the Brown Water Navy, Task Force 116, Black Beret, Vietnam and Cambodia in 1970. I pulled over 325 night patrols.

Remember each sunrise: This line means a lot to me, because it meant that I had survived another night patrol on the Baasac and Mekong Rivers. During the invasion of Cambodia, April 29, 1970, my

36' L.C.V.P. led all of the larger vessels up the Mekong River as we passed into Cambodia.

Night-day, night-day relieved by Swift boat with sonar. My L.C.V.P. went shore to shore, upriver. Dropping a lead-line to mark the channel and looking for mines. As the U.S. Army and A.R.V.N. attack C.O.S.V.N. by ground. My weapon was a 12 gauge riot gun 7 shot double 00 Buck shot.

I am 100 percent disabled with PTSD, total and permanent! Eaten-up with Agent Orange.

Raymond W. Enstine, Jr.
Sergeant, USA, A Battery 1/82 Artillery Americal Div,
Vietnam, 1969–1970

When I returned from Vietnam, I realized that I had problems with survivor guilt and I had not grieved for my friends who were left behind in Vietnam. Finally, after 20 years, I got myself into a Vet Center counseling group where I began to explore and understand why I had "numbed out" and I began working toward recovery from my PTSD.

One of the techniques frequently used to put one in touch with his or her feelings is psychodrama. In our therapy group, many of us had not sufficiently grieved for our dead or wounded buddies or even the loss of our own youth. One night, the therapist had us hold a funeral service for our dead comrades. The group was held in the chapel of a local airforce base, so we needed few props to set the mood. We each picked one person to represent all our dead friends, and then we were asked to say good-bye to the individual. We took turns, one representing the dead on the altar, and the other talking to the dead buddy. It was very difficult for us.

Later that year, the Vet Center sponsored a bus trip to the Wall in Washington. Four from my group decided to go together and try to finally "let our dead buddies go." It was a very spiritual experience for us all. As we looked up the names of friends on the wall, we would also find names of others we had forgotten. My buddy from the funeral ceremony and I were surprised when we found the names, together, side by side, of the two buddies we had picked to say good-bye to a few months earlier. Twenty years of tears were finally released and a heavy weight began to lift.

On the way home, I finally accepted that my buddies were dead, and that they were safe because they were together. I wrote this poem—"Back to Back"—to capture my feelings, so I could look back in later years and remember them as closely as possible. It was a very spiritual experience for me as I was finally able to let go. The Wall will always be a special place to me and I will always look at my visit as a turning point in my recovery. A copy of the poem hangs in the Vet Center and is used to close sessions on grieving.

· JAMES S BURNETT Jr ·

· JERRY LEE O'NEAL ·

Back to Back

Fear, our constant shadow, pulling from behind
Trusting a buddy's back, helping calm the mind
Watching for each other, exchanging sacred trust
Humanity in Vietnam, it came to mean so much

Back in the world, twenty years have passed
New buddies, but old memories last
Traveling to the Wall, emotions back to back
Searching resolution, separating fear from fact

Coming upon the Wall, trying again to say good-bye
Tears and joy flow cleansingly, from buddies survived
Surprised, we find their names, Jimmy and Jerry Lee are safe
They're watching back to back, our hearts relieved by fate?

Ken Sauvage
Corporal, USMC, 2nd Bn 3rd Marines,
Vietnam, 1968–1969

Counseling has enabled me to choose what I do with the emotions and energy that periodically well up in me because of my Vietnam experience. Because I can now look, talk, write, draw, and cry about these things, my orientation to the experiences has changed. Slowly over the years, I have looked at and responded to different aspects of the trauma (from philosophical thoughts to concrete memories) trying to understand what happened to me—to us—politically, militarily, socially, and morally.

When I first discovered that the pain I had been feeling over the years had a name, and that many other people who had shared similar experiences in Vietnam were also sharing similar symptoms now, the sense of isolation was literally lifted off of my soul. This was replaced by a sense of belonging, sharing, identification. Just knowing I wasn't alone, that I shared these feelings with others, and that the pain had root causes is an incredible feeling. I am not saying that all Vietnam veterans are alike. We all come from different backgrounds, served in different units, in different areas, at different times. But in spite of the differences, I can still find commonalties in how we impose meaning onto those experiences.

Vietnam

John Almeida
Vietnam

Vietnam, Vietnam, Vietnam, you seduced my mind
Into believing in death and killing
Oh, maybe you couldn't have achieved your mission
Had I not wanted it so bad—
I was young and impressionable then, and you took
Advantage of my youth.
With all the God stuff that I'd learned that didn't seem to
Be working for me,
The lure of your devilish ways suited me fine.
Without any remorse, I caressed your ideals
With open arms
And I enjoyed my brief swim through your deceptiveness.
You gave me a sense of reality that made my life seem real.
You spoiled me with your climate and untamed wilderness.
You tempted me with an on-the-edge way to exist.
Caught up in the rapture and freedom you allowed,
Nothing mattered but the moment, and I embraced Death.

But you didn't devour me forever, Demon that you were!
"I'm Baaack!" you say from time to time.
And that's okay 'cause I don't care if you are anymore;
I know now there's no need to be upset and beat you off with a
stick.
You may be unpleasant for a while, but you will soon wear off.
So you're back? So what! I can live with you now.

Dana S.
1st Lieutenant, USA Nurse Corps, Vietnam

One of the only places I feel that I can fully acknowledge my status as a veteran and my overwhelming pain and confusion about the war is at the Wall. At the Vietnam Veterans Memorial I am the one, finally, who belongs; everyone who didn't serve personally or surrender a loved one to the war is a mere bystander. At the Wall I don't have to hide or explain my emotions. I don't have to translate my vocabulary. Even though tears may course down my cheeks, I feel the lines in my face ease as the chronic stress of keeping up appearances wanes. At the Wall I can be at peace with everything I am, and with everything I remember.

Going to the Wall is a necessary periodic ritual for me. Even if one has been saved, one still needs to go to church. Even if the funeral is over, one still needs to visit the cemetery. Even if one has said good-bye, one sometimes needs to say hello again. I try to visit the Wall when the crowds are sparse but when there are other vets around. It is then that I can pay my respects, revalidate old memories, and soothe a few of the restless spirits that always seem to keep me company. The Wall reminds me of war's greatest lesson: that of the utter preciousness and fragility of life. It is there that I can make strides toward healing.

At the Wall my husband is impatient with this need. He gets cold; he gets hungry; he wants to leave long before I feel ready. He can't see me doing anything, and I can't verbalize what it is that I'm doing. Nevertheless, it needs to be done. I suspect a lot of other veterans' spouses are similarly bewildered by the power of this impulse of veterans simply to "be with the Wall." There are also may "tree vets" who spend time close to the Wall but cannot approach closer than the trees south of the Wall. Yet they, too, are seeking to share their pain and memory with others like them. It is hard for a civilian to understand that the veteran who looks at the Wall sees and talks to people who are visible only to other vets. It is difficult to understand that the veteran who touches the Wall touches emotions she or he may have access to nowhere else in time or space. It is hard to understand that the veteran who is enveloped by the Wall has entered a sacred reality that can never fully include any current loved one. But the Wall is powerful medicine. It takes powerful medicine to heal such a mighty hurt. And some of us veterans will need to stand embraced within the healing aura of the Wall a long, long time.

Duane A. "Tubby" Brudvig
Specialist/5, USA, Vietnam, 1969-1970

PTSD has eaten at me for years and it is just recently that I'm starting to get over it. The tenth anniversary of the fall of Vietnam was a terrible time, because it brought all this stuff back again. I have done some constructive things like help locate old members of my unit for reunions and started writing a book about my experiences. I've written some stories for other authors and I've stayed in touch with friends who needed to have someone to talk to when they were down. Now that I have stopped drinking, maybe I can help others with their drinking problems!

The most helpful aspect of my therapy is being able to talk with others who were going through the same feelings I was, and expressing truthfully my feelings without worrying that I am making someone feel uncomfortable.

R. Bruce Johnson
E-4, USA, 4/3 Inf 196th Light Inf Americal Division,
101st Airborne Div, Vietnam, 1969-1971

Everything started for me early, hearing my father talk of W.W. II, speaking of the great bravery shown and of a job well done. I remember him talking of his homecoming and of a grateful nation. I wished this in time for myself. I wondered if my turn would come, the time to prove myself in the face of death. I wanted to serve and fight for my country just as my dad did. I remember hearing of Korea and the French in Vietnam. I wondered if this could be my chance. I enlisted in the Army and it wasn't long before I got my wish. At this time there wasn't a lot of protesting; or if there was, I didn't hear much of it until later. I served to the best of my ability and was proud, for a brief period of time anyway.

The return home was lonely. I can remember the fear of battle, the aching look in friends' eyes, the screams of pain, and the fear of the unknown that stays with a soldier. It never goes away. The faces of friends who died, and the shame of not remembering their names; yet their faces are there all the time. The hidden guilt that when I left, I let people down: people who were my friends, people who were going to die. Facing the shame of crying (and doing this in private), not wanting family or friends to see me. Always trying to explain to an unconcerned public until I gave up and held everything within. This is all part of PTSD.

I came back to an uncaring public. What did they know of war, especially of the war we fought? It was nothing I expected. We dealt with bugs, booby traps, tunnels, and disease. There hardly ever was territory to take. We fought an unseen enemy. But through all this, we did our job with pride.

On my return home, I was spat on. I just wanted to forget, to get away from my feelings. I wanted to be proud, but people made me ashamed. I wanted respect, all I got was called names. I turned to drugs and alcohol and developed an attitude. I think though, that these bad times really helped to shape me today. I dealt with nightmares, seeing faces but not being able to put names to them. The pain was growing in intensity, not only mental but physical. I was diagnosed with pancreatic cancer and my stomach and one-half of my pancreas were removed.

I still suffer the effects of this but over the years I have learned that, even though that part of my life can never be forgotten, it can be endured. Through treatment I have been off drugs and alcohol for 15 years. Even though the faces of war are still there, I can cope. I can shed tears without being ashamed and I don't have to be alone. I have learned to talk and bring things out in the open.

A vet can now share what used to be private, and by doing so he can help himself and others. We are just veterans of war like any other and we can be proud of the job we did. We don't have to be ashamed or apologize for our actions.

I have learned that a returning vet should be deprogrammed. He shouldn't have to fight one day and be home the next. And he definitely should not have to bear the scars of war alone. Seeing our brothers killed or maimed or having to kill isn't easy, but now we can face this together. Nam vets have each other and by being together, we can heal ourselves. We can go on with our lives. Remember that there is no shame in crying (and that family and friends have wide shoulders). Once we have healed ourselves we can then work on the nation.

Vietnam Journey

Raymond W. Enstine, Jr.
Sergeant, USA, A Battery 1/82 Artillery Americal Div,
Vietnam, 1969–1970

Left our world Thanksgiving 1969
  Vietnam, land of contradictions, bewildered
  this soldier's mind
My feelings were quick-frozen by fear, guilt, and pain
  Numb, I survived, a robot, living day to day
Days pass to E.T.S. and my bodily escape
  My feelings increasingly distant, with less intensity and shape

Night flight returns my body, feelings float far away
  Numb, craving solitude, fabricating crises every day
Can't admit Vietnam's realities to anyone, most of all myself
  Guilt fuels quests for memorials to friendships,
  grievings unfelt
Life's pace quickens daily, I search for internal peace
  Satisfaction and resolution seem so far from reach

Others help, I begin to feel, troubling memories become moot
  Pushing back thru unowned feelings,
  encountering kinder truths
A journey to the Wall soothes saying good-byes
  Looking thru pain and tears, radiates joy and pride
Life again has color, the future now seems bright
  At last I feel I'm home, Happiness now mine!!!

Vet Center

Thomas N. "Tommy" Bills
Sergeant, USA, 2/7th Cav (Gary Owen Bde) 1st Cav Div
Vietnam

A Time to Heal

E. Michael Helms
Corporal, USMC, Vietnam

Sometimes the healing process can be as painful as the wounding.

I felt uneasy, exposed, like being on point and forced by the lay of the terrain to cross 200 meters of open rice paddy. But this was 10,000 miles and 20 years removed from Nam.

I swallowed hard and choked back the tears. I was about to reveal for the first time the awful truth about the horrible, senseless death of my closest buddy in Vietnam. I squirmed in my chair and stared across the small room where Vet Center counselor Gregg Brown sat patiently. "Go ahead. Just relax and take your time."

It had taken more than a year of group and one-on-one counseling to bring me to this point. I had hooked up with the Tallahassee Vet Center outreach program through the recommendation of a concerned friend/case worker employed with the local county Veterans Service Office. Though the initial interview and first few sessions had been somewhat strained and uncomfortable (after all, who can trust anyone who works for the government?) Gregg, a Vietnam vet himself, soon put me at ease. Before long I knew he could be counted on to "cover my back." He had earned my trust and I began to open up to him.

After several months of talking through my combat experiences, a long-ignored desire to write my story was rekindled. My counselor greeted this idea with enthusiasm, thinking that this "journaling" would be a significant step forward in my therapy. I didn't realize the intensity of the experience that would follow.

Gregg was surprised when I showed him the first two completed chapters of my "book" at our next session. He had heard similar vows dozens of times from other vets and seen them come to nothing. He promised me an unprejudiced critique of my effort and I assured him chapter three would soon be ready.

We both delivered. Gregg could see that I was really serious about working through my problems, and I could tell that he had a genuine interest in helping me. From that time on our relationship deepened. In my book I tell the story as though it is unfolding at the present moment through the eyes and mind of the 18- or 19-year-old Marine I was then. In order to do that, I had to get back "into character," in essence. I had to become that teenage warrior again, and psych myself into reliving Vietnam as it happened.

Re-experiencing the Nam was intense and painful. It almost totally consumed me but was very eye-opening. In the years since the war, I had sometimes found myself missing, even longing for, that incredible "rush" that came with combat. I yearned to recapture that feeling of being "really alive." But as is often the case in such matters, the years had hidden the "dark side," the absolute sickening cold terror that would grip my bowels like a vice when the rounds began to hiss and snap. As I got into character and became that young grunt again, I learned anew what fear was all about. God, I was in for another tour, but this time I would have to grind it out on paper, knowing and dreading what lay ahead.

As the "written tour" progressed it became more and more difficult to continue. Daily I was dredging up old ghosts and painful
wounds. I would find myself at the end of a day's writing shaken, my
heart pounding and my nerves shot. My sleep became increasingly fit-
ful, and I began relying far too often on a six-pack or two to calm myself down and just numb out. My family life was suffering. I could see
the pain and confusion in the eyes of my wife, and especially my
daughters. I began to distance myself from them, although I knew it
was hurting them. Their pain was like a bayonet in my gut.

Still, I was determined to see it through, I had to exorcise these
horrors that had been haunting me for so many years. I found myself
fighting back the tears and telling Gregg in a broken, halting voice
what I never told anyone. About how we had been under so much
stress from weeks and weeks of constant fighting during Tet; how we
were all so weary, so completely worn out, and just waiting for the big
push by the NVA to overrun and wipe us out. About how we were getting ready to go out on another LP for the night when it just happened,
so suddenly: the quick exchange of words, and then "T" must have just
lost it, just snapped, because suddenly he chambered a round right
there in the hooch, pointed the '16 at "B" and pulled the trigger. About
how "B" was slammed down, then bounced up crazily on his knees,
teetering to and fro like a Jack-in-the-box, the terrible throaty groan
and the pleading eyes which silently screamed out to me for help until
they rolled back in the sockets and he fell over dead. About the helplessness I felt, the utter senselessness, the horror of it all.

And then one day the book was finished. Ironically, it had taken
13 months to write. In my mind this seemed to make up for the tour I
had never completed in Vietnam (I had been medevaced out with not
quite half my tour completed). Gregg was with me, encouraging and
guiding me throughout the entire painful process. Along the way,
things that for so long had been clouded began to clear.

Gregg explained that after I witnessed "B's" death, I experienced
a "psychic overload." I simply numbed out and became essentially an
"automaton"; I quit feeling or caring or hoping, and was just waiting
my turn to die. He suggested that that was why I had such little recall
of the following month when my outfit moved to the Cua Viet River
area and was nearly wiped out in the fighting during Operation
Napoleon-Saline. For years, he explained, I had been suffering from
the effects of PTSD.

It was as if a veil had fallen from my eyes, and a 1,000 pound rucksack had been lifted off my back. It all made sense! I wasn't crazy after all. There was an explanation for all the blank spots. I didn't need to feel guilty anymore for things that had happened—or didn't happen—over which I had no control. Bad things do happen, and often to good people.

I will be forever grateful to the Vet Center program, and to Gregg Brown in particular. He helped me see, over the course of nearly three years, that Vietnam doesn't have to dominate my life anymore. It happened, and the painful memories will always be with me. But now I can put them into perspective. Vietnam was not my entire life; it was only a season in my life. The bleakness of winter will give way to the promise of spring, as surely as day follows night. And healing will come, if we let it.

In the Name of War/In the Name of Peace

Samuel D.
Sergeant, USMC, HMM-362 "Ugly Angels,"
Vietnam, 1968–1969

In the name of war
I wasn't suppose to care
About how you felt inside
Or your reasons for being there

In the name of war
I did my job so well
But my training didn't prepare me
For how it feels to kill

In the name of war
Your lives I did end
But given different circumstances
I might have called you friend

But, in the name of peace
I've longed to say to you

I'm sorry for all the things
That soldiers train to do

In the name of peace
I would also like to say
I promise to never forget you
Until my dying day

And finally, in the name of peace
Had our roles been reversed
I know God and I would forgive you
As long as you forgave yourself first

———

Charles Felix
Corporal, USMC, W.W. II:
Bougainville, Guam, Iwo Jima

Some five percent of my life was spent in the military and only about one-half of that in combat, but it was the most impressionable period of my life. I fought as a Marine in the Pacific and served with a ship-to-shore fire control team in the Solomons. This included a landing on Vella Lavella and the harrowing sinking of a ship while returning to Guadalcanal. I made beachhead landings with the 3rd Marine Division on Bougainville, Guam, and Iwo Jima. I suppose I came home with guilt feelings because of the incredible number of young men who died while I seemed blessed with immunity in combat. A half-century later I still have frightened dreams of combat. I suppose virtually every morning since then I have awakened on Iwo Jima. Iwo was a slaughterhouse but it has subsequently helped in life. Regardless of any adversity I face, I have always noted that "Iwo was worse." Friends and family seem to find it humorous, but I believe the experience of Iwo Jima made it easier to cope with life, and in truth, Iwo was worse. I have gone through therapy twice and can't say that it has helped a lot. But the best medicine I have encountered has been to write about those young men who did not return.

I still don't understand why I lived and so many fine young men died. I still weep for them and many has been the time when I lay awake in the quiet hours of darkness and thought how cruel life was to them but good to me. Bottling it up inside never helped, but to remember and to write has helped bring peace.

The Shadow of War

Daryl S. Paulson, Ph.D.
Sergeant, USMC, 5th Marine Regiment,
An Hoa, Vietnam, 1968–1969

It wasn't long after joining the Marine Corps that I realized the magnitude of my decision. I'd never really thought the enemy would shoot back. When I saw combat footage during infantry training, I realized that being killed in Vietnam was very probable.

I learned of the horrors of war within my first two weeks of combat. Our radioman, who was just in front of me, was shot through the head. He was simply "tagged" and "bagged," just like that, he was gone. Several days later, I saw 17 of my comrades, who were coming in on a helicopter ground assault, killed by direct hit of a 121-mm rocket. At the end of those two weeks, six seasoned veterans were destroyed by an incoming mortar round while they ate their C-rations. Just like that, they too were gone.

I continually witnessed young friend after friend brutally killed. I was also changing. I was becoming increasingly numb—a true fighting machine. I killed Viet Cong and North Vietnamese Army regularly, as if they mattered no more than rats. I enjoyed their suffering and pain but deep inside, I knew I was wounded, that I had become an animal. I wondered if I would ever again meet a friendly person, one who would not try to kill me.

Finally, I was going home. I felt a tremendous sense of relief and was determined to get on with my life. I enrolled in college, but life in the United States was not what I expected. During the entire 13 months that I was in Vietnam, I fantasized about returning, finding that special woman, and devoting my life to her. But at home, I didn't feel comfortable with women; they made me nervous. Being held by a woman made me feel vulnerable; I was terribly sad and afraid in her arms.

Later, I discovered drinking made relationships with women easier; I did not feel vulnerable and could use them for sex.

Other areas of my life changed, too. I had trouble sleeping. I'd be tired but as soon as I tried to sleep, I found myself wide awake. I'd become fearful, waiting for something to happen but it made no sense. Why can't I sleep? What's wrong?

One day I had an anxiety attack; suddenly I felt I was dying. My heart began to pound; I grew dizzy and my eyes wouldn't focus. I began gasping for breath and sweating profusely. I freaked out. The doctor examined me but could find nothing physically wrong. To me, this meant something very serious was wrong. I became increasingly fearful. I felt I was losing control, near death, just as I'd felt in Vietnam. Everywhere I went and everything I did was enmeshed with fear and dread of an imminent catastrophe. After experiencing about five more panic attacks, my doctor sent me to a psychiatrist.

I saw my emotional problems as proof of my weakness, but went to the psychiatrist because I needed relief from this new form of suffering. I told him about Vietnam, but he wasn't interested. Instead, he prescribed two tranquilizers and an anti-depressant and told me to take it easy; I continued slipping into a pit of despair.

Distraught and depressed as I was, I tried to go on picnics with my friends, but the fear hounded me. I couldn't enjoy myself, even while using tranquilizers. I felt so uneasy, so vulnerable. In the mountains, where we took our outings, I watched for enemy hiding in the trees, stalking me, just like in Vietnam. As time went on, I took not only the tranquilizers, but also a bottle of whiskey and a gun. I could tolerate the outings if I was drunk.

It wasn't long before a new fear developed—thunderstorms. Even though I knew thunder wasn't a rocket attack, the sound returned me to Vietnam. The storms set off such panic I could not be calmed for several days, even on tranquilizers and alcohol.

That wasn't all. I began questioning my involvement in Vietnam. When I finally realized that there was no purpose to the war other than getting many good men killed, my entire life collapsed. I could only suffer and drink. I was afraid and plagued with guilt. I tried to find a place to go for acceptance and forgiveness, to get out of my hell. I tried church, but it didn't work. I felt too guilty; I had injured and killed my fellow human beings with delight. No, I could not go to church, I had too much blood on my hands. No one wanted me, not even God. I had killed his children.

I felt completely alone and isolated in life. It was as if I lived in an alien world within which I couldn't communicate. I could not share my pain and fear with anyone. I spent most of my time alone, drinking, trying to assuage the pain of my life's meaninglessness. One night, I found my way out. A loaded .38 caliber revolver. I could end my suffering in a flash by sending one 158 grain hollow point bullet into my brain.

As I looked at the gun, for some reason, I thought about Job's suffering in the Bible and how it had been for a purpose. I thought of my comrades who had been killed and the despair they would feel with no one to tell their story. I made a vow to myself to stay drunk until I found someone who could help me. After going through four psychotherapists, I finally found one who was not only competent but who genuinely cared about me.

But I soon found therapy worse than the actual combat. I had to experience the terrors of war again and again in the therapist's office. I had to face tremendous guilt from what I had done and how willing I had been to do it. For example, I decided to give myself a 21st birthday present by getting a body count of 21. But on my 21st birthday, I had killed only twenty and one half NVA. I wounded one of them and someone else killed him, so I only got a half a credit. I had to face incidents like this. Now I knew how the Nazis were able to kill millions of Jews. It was the same as with me—following orders.

I spent three painful years in psychotherapy just to become functional, reclaiming my life, molecule by molecule. But I hung in and climbed out of the shadow of war. Then I spent another 10 years in therapy working on improving the quality of my life.

Today, 25 years after being in combat, I still feel a vague sense of lurking danger, but it is nothing compared to the past. After service in Vietnam, I know that death is but a heartbeat away. But there is a positive side to my story. From my Vietnam experience, I learned how to continue on in spite of pain. I have found this to be very advantageous in my professional life. After having worked unhappily for the same company for 10 years, I took the situation into my own hands. With but $3,297.00 to my name, I began my own company. Today, two-and-a-half years later, my company employs 18 people in three locations. I doubt whether I could have endured the fear of undertaking this venture had I not gone to Vietnam.

Second Lieutenant
Clebe McClary
United States
MARINES

Lt. Clebe McClary

Sgt. Richard G. Lawrence
Combat Vietnam Veteran,
USMC

Editors' note: Clebe McClary, an inspiration to the artist,
lost his arm and eye to grenade and satchel charge explosions
during hand-to-hand combat with a North Vietnamese suicide squad.
A platoon leader with the 1st Recon Battalion, 1st Marine Division,
he received both Silver and Bronze Stars, and three Purple Hearts
for wounds that required 34 operations. Inspired by a sermon at
a gospel rally, Lt. McClary committed his life to motivate others
by sharing his personal faith in God. His inspirational message
has been recognized by people as diverse as the
Rev. Billy Graham, Dodgers manager Tommy LaSorda,
Cowboy's coach Tom Landry, and others in major industry.

———

Robert di G.
Private First Class, USA, Vietnam, 1969

I accept the money from the VA for my disability as what I am due. It isn't quite like the 160 acres the veterans received for fighting the Revolutionary War, but it keeps the wolves away. May God have mercy on us all.

———

Dana S.
1st Lieutenant, USA Nurse Corps, Vietnam

Gradually I was able to dwell less and less upon my direct Vietnam experience and address more current concerns, though in the context of my identity as a veteran. I'm learning what place being a Vietnam veteran has in my emotional structure, as well as how my status as a veteran influences my attitudes, beliefs, and interactions with others.

I'm learning to give Vietnam its due without letting it monopolize my life. After years of therapy I've come to realize that the goal of therapy cannot be to make Vietnam go away. Neither a great therapist, nor prayer, nor the love of a spouse, nor hoping for a better past can make it go away. Vietnam was an unmitigated tragedy, and nothing can change that. What therapy can do is make the past bearable by enabling me to formulate some meaning from the experience. Through therapy I am learning to accept the fact that I will never be the same person as before I went. I will always be more serious and less spontaneous than I would have been had I not gone. And of course, until the day I die I will always carry with me the images of those who never made it back, or might have, if only . . . . Yes, I still have a big stack of unopened, unanswered "if onlys" to go through.

Even so, I try to tell myself that I must be a good person who is worthy of life and happiness. Would a bad person feel this much pain for this long? I believe that, ironically, in my capacity to suffer lies the path back to a more human, less agonized existence. And to the occasional widow or mother or orphan huddled in the shadow of the Wall who asks me, "Was there anyone over there who cared?" I can answer with a resounding "Yes!"

Duane A. "Tubby" Brudvig
Specialist/5, USA, Vietnam, 1969–1970

I kept thinking about Nam all the time. Now I deal with it by talking to people about it. Vets will come up to me and talk about some of their experiences. I have a cause now, so I try to help the best I can by talking with others.

David A. Somerville
Sergeant, USA, 2/502 Inf Bn 101st Airborne Div Hq Co,
Camp Eagle, Vietnam, 1970–1971

At one time I used to say that all those guys died for nothing. Now I know better. Any man that lays down his life so others can be free is not only rich, I believe he sits at God's right hand.

Obituary

Robert E. Bennett
Captain, USA, Vietnam

Defending the DMZ cost us years in Korea. It cost us 58,000 lives in Vietnam. The hippies didn't win the big one but they screwed us up, along with their friend Hanoi Jane (who has since mended her ways). We needed the Mujahadeen (Islamic freedom fighters in Afghanistan) and the freedom fighters in East Germany, Poland, Czechoslovakia, and Hungary to do it but we did it! The Soviet colossus is dead. And, that's some of the best treatment for PTSD you can get!

Reflections

James F. Sedgley
Platoon Sergeant, USA, 1st Plt Co E 184th Inf Reg 7th Inf Div,
W.W. II: Aleutian Islands, Kwajalein, Philippines, Okinawa

In 1988, I requested assistance from the Placer County Board of Supervisors for the creation of a "Memorial to All Veterans." This they gave, with the assistance of the local veteran groups: the VFW, DAV, American Legion, the Fleet Reserve and their auxiliaries. It is now a reality. Spearheading this effort gave me much personal satisfaction. It gave me confidence to pursue a goal and the impetus to try and improve the lot of all veterans. I now belong to the first three groups listed above.

From these memberships, and their monthly magazines, I have learned much regarding the definition and the newer approach to the treatment of the mental wounds of war. I appreciate the long awaited designation and realistic "nom de guerre"—Post Traumatic Stress Disorder. PTSD sure beats the category of "Nervous Disorder," circa 1945. The term is more definitive and carries much less stigma. If we had been accurately diagnosed earlier, we might have had a more rewarding life; without the post-trauma we have endured for these four decades and more.

I was stricken—and
missed my chance—for
a normal life—now
too old to dance!

Paul Cohen, MSW
Specialist/4, USA, 2nd Bn 16th Inf Bde 1st Inf Div,
Vietnam, 1967–1968

Fathers: the men who raise us, shape our beliefs, and values. Fathers: our leaders, those we look up to, who we follow. Fathers: our culture, society, and government, those who make laws, policies, and give us our missions.

My grandfather served in W.W. I, my father in W.W. II, and so when I first heard of Vietnam the only worry I had was that it wouldn't last long enough for me to get my chance. This was 1964, I was 15, and as it turned out I had nothing to worry about, I was going to get what I wanted . . . and more. I joined the Army, volunteering for the infantry and Nam, the day of my 18th birthday in 1967. I landed at Tan Son Nhut on Thanksgiving day of that same year. I was in a hurry, I felt I had something to prove back then. I had a mission, a purpose: I was going to serve my country, be a hero, maybe win a fistful of medals, but more importantly, have my father be proud of me. I would have done anything to win his approval.

As a therapist and a Vietnam vet recovering from PTSD, I find my work with other vets has a dual focus. Eliciting memories and feelings of the actual combat trauma is a very important piece of the work, essential to getting past the block, getting the vet "unstuck" and moving on with his life. The other piece involves fathers, in all their various forms. I see Vietnam, and subsequently PTSD, as having this dual edge of trauma/content and trauma/context. My recovery and my work revolve around integrating both pieces.

I wasn't always a therapist. When I came back home from Nam at the age of 19, flat on my back after walking into an ambush as a pointman and getting part of my leg shot off, I thought my mission was over. I wanted to get a job, get married, have kids, live a normal life. Things, I found, would never be simple for me. Little by little I felt myself slipping away, and not even caring.

Problem? I didn't have a problem! I got angrier and angrier. I began using drugs, marijuana, ups, downs, whatever. Alcohol, too. Then together. Problem? Maybe you got a problem, I'm doing just fine! I didn't need anyone, I didn't trust anyone. Well, yes, there was this one little problem. All the drugs, all the booze in the world couldn't stop the nightmares, the thoughts, the pain. I began getting violent, breaking things, terrorizing my wife and kids. Losing jobs.

One day I got so angry (as usual over something stupid and trivial), I thought I was going to kill someone. Enraged and out of control, I really needed to hurt someone, anyone. I got my Swiss Army knife (the knife with a hundred uses) and I locked myself in the bathroom. I stared at myself in the mirror; I stared at the knife; and then slowly and calmly, I began cutting myself on the chest. It hurt, but it calmed me down. I had taken my internal pain and externalized it. I was in control again and I had taken that control by punishing myself, by finally getting in touch with my shame, my sense of failure. I had let them down:

my father, all of them. They had given me a mission and I had failed. And they, in turn, had betrayed me.

I didn't figure all that out right then. It took years and years of therapy, of finding the right people. I was diagnosed with major depression, bi-polar disorder, maybe even psychosis. I was given drugs, even after I freely admitted my substance abuse. The weekend of my final breakdown I had been using cocaine, marijuana, beer, 100 proof vodka, Xanax, Navane, Klonopin, and Trilafon. I reported to work Monday morning, on time, ever efficient, and felt so . . . empty . . . so . . . numb. I went into the locker room, took out my trusty P38 can opener and tried to open a wrist. Some of the guys walked in and grabbed it from me. I jumped up and began punching holes in the walls. They finally subdued me and rushed me to the emergency room. I answered all their inane questions, feeling detached and bored, not caring, and eventually found myself locked up in a 30-day drug and alcohol program. Every time I mentioned Vietnam they said I was an addict. They wouldn't let me talk about Vietnam, they said it had nothing to do with my problem, I was an addict, an alcoholic. I left clean and sober but still empty, hurting, angry, and ashamed. Eventually, I went to a VA Hospital as an outpatient.

I was then admitted as an inpatient. First on a locked, general admission ward, then finally I was interviewed and admitted to the PTSD program. This was 1988, 20 years after I had come home from Nam. They told me I had PTSD and I would have it for the rest of my life so I had better quit complaining and whining and learn how to live with it. And that was the beginning of my recovery. What I had, had a name. It wasn't me, it had been done to me, and what I could do now was to live in spite of it. I could not go back and erase what happened. Like a diabetic, I could learn to live with it.

But first I had to find something to live for. I needed a mission. I found my mission at the Wall. I went the first time with the local chapter of the VVA, another part of my recovery. I finally found someone to talk to about Nam, other vets, and together we tried to heal ourselves based on the knowledge the doctors gave us, or what we read, what we heard, what we saw. Like the Wall. I remember going to look for familiar but long forgotten names. I scanned the black stone and saw one there, and there, and there, and suddenly every name I saw was familiar; I knew them all. My individual experience was transcended by something much, much bigger. And I cried. I cried for all those who were lost, wasted. All those sons and brothers and boyfriends and husbands. The lives they could have lived, the contributions they could have made but didn't, and here I was, a survivor. I was living, I was given the chance they didn't get, and I was wasting it. Their waste could be forgiven because they did not know, but I was wasting purposefully. Then I was struck with the thought that I could give purpose to their sacrifice. I could give meaning to what had happened by learning from it and helping others with that knowledge. I knew I finally had a true mission, one I could accomplish and be proud of. I may have been let down by my fathers, my mission betrayed, but I could not be part of their conspiracy of silence.

A group of other Vietnam vets and I began lecturing and showing slides of Vietnam to local school children. Not war stories, but what it felt like to be 18, alone, afraid, and far from home. I continued to take control of that which had for over 20 years controlled me. I also went back to college and graduated with honors. I went on to graduate school and got my Masters. I became a therapist to try to help others sort out their own pain, to find some meaning in what has happened to them, to help them find their mission as I finally found my own.

Clyde Q.
Corporal, USMC (R),
South Korea, 1950–1951

God bless those who are enduring PTSD, and may their wounded memories soon be healed.

My Wall

Jerry Osby "Doc" Anderson
E-4, USA, Americal Division, Duc Pho, Vietnam, 1967-1968

When I left Vietnam in November 1968 and came home to a society that rejected veterans, I brought a wall with me. Not knowing why my wall was around me, I used it to block myself off from society for 23 years. Inside my wall are intrusive thoughts that lead to flashbacks. The smell, the screams, the fixed eyeballs that stay with me all the time, the pleas for help from dying men, blood, guts, crippling, death, body bags, mortars, mines, snipers. Mental wounds that society can't see are among the worst, and I have kept my wall around them. Being a medic was one hell of a job for a 20-year-old kid from Georgia.

Sometimes I had to decide who, out of three or more wounded men, I would try to save. I had to decide who had the best chance to live and leave the rest there to die. That left me with one hell of a guilt trip. Deep down in my heart, I know I was a damn good medic and I did the best I could.

In my wall there were five rules of survival: eat, sleep, sex, fight, and flee. There was no communication in my wall. Distrust for our government and society was a big problem in my wall. Alcohol was a big problem in my relationships and jobs. PTSD and alcohol together make one hell of a problem. I had to get treatment for alcohol first, before I could deal with PTSD. After eight months sober I started getting nervous, not wanting to go to AA meetings, not wanting to be around people, withdrawing from society, I wanted to be alone.

I sat around for three months behind my wall, then a buddy asked me if I wanted to go up to the Atlanta Vet Center. I knew if I didn't do something I would be back where I started. I am now in treatment for PTSD with alcohol and drug addiction and it really has been working for me. Just talking with veterans helps me a lot. Writing and listening to other veterans really helps. Writing about my wall (with tears in my eyes) is good for me. These are tears of joy, for my wall is falling down.

I found out my wall doesn't have to be so high. I am also learning how to deal with the wall society has built to separate itself from Vietnam veterans. To all veterans and families or anybody suffering with the four Ds—Death, Destruction, Discomfort, Divorce—there is help that works if you want it to.

We are waiting for you with open arms.

Duane A. "Tubby" Brudvig
Specialist/5, USA, Vietnam, 1969-1970

My world looked promising, but the older I got the more difficult it seemed at times. I turned to God many times and I know He understood everything, but He wanted me to figure it out for myself.

I used to have a hard time with the MIA/POW issue. When I was in Germany, my last gunner was shot down in Laos, and listed as missing in action. I was so far away and there was nothing I could do. Later, I became active in trying to get the Vietnamese to release our POWs. I started petitions in our work place, wrote letters to congressmen and the President, and flew an MIA/POW flag at our shop. Every time I heard something about the issue I got my hopes up, only to be let down. After drinking too much, I would cry. Now I've learned that there are some things that God has to handle. All I can do is pray.

Sharing the Struggles of a Friend

George Hill
Corporal, USMC, Vietnam, 1967–1969

I met Gary seven and a half years ago when we and five or six other combat vets were in a "closed group" at the Jacksonville Veterans Outreach Center. We were acquaintances, not real good friends yet. Most of us had had 50 jobs or more, numerous attempts at relationships, an inability to cope with events of Vietnam and a history of severe and chronic readjustment problems—a typical "rap group."

Gary was above average in talent, as are many Vietnam vets, but he had come to a point where he desperately needed peace of mind in his life. He needed to put the war experience in perspective in order to continue. After a year or so the members of our group went their separate ways but several of us kept in contact. Gary and I occasionally saw each other as we struggled through our separate lives. Our group had a common, sad theme: suicide, jail sentences, continuous psychiatric hospitalizations, etc. When I hit bottom, I sought and received help through the Gainesville VA Medical Center, and then further treatment at PTSD units in St. Petersburg, FL and Augusta, GA.

Gary was extremely bitter toward the government after being refused help with his Agent Orange problems. Frustration over numerous jobs made him self-destructive. We talked and saw each other more often and I tried many times to get him to seek help. Finally, at a reunion of Florida Vietnam vets, he said, "Man, I gotta get help," and told me how unbearable his life had become; how he could not let go of certain incidents that had been bothering him for a quarter of a century. Gary asked me, "Man, walk me through." I understood.

A week later I took him to the VA. He was surprised when I introduced him to certain people who cared about his condition. He began weekly therapy. I looked forward to going to Jacksonville to get him every week. He was living with his mother and she told me that she was glad he was finally getting help. He would stay one or two nights a week in my room; we talked and shared a lot. We became very close.

After several months, I could see some changes in his behavior. He seemed to have some hope. He applied for the Bay Pines PTSD recovery unit in St. Petersburg. Having completed that program three years earlier, I was familiar with the program and the staff. I introduced him; he was accepted, and started the program two weeks later.

I visited Gary in the second week of the eight-week program. He was depressed about some of the painful experiences that had to be addressed and processed in therapy, but Gary was really up about receiving help after all his years of struggling. He really liked his doctor and the unit staff. He had never before been anyplace where people empathized with his problems relating to Vietnam. A few days later, when we drove through the large veterans cemetery on the hospital grounds, Gary told me that he'd broken down a couple days earlier as taps was being played during a POW recognition ceremony. We agreed that I'd pick him up the next weekend for his weekend pass, and Gary said, "Man, you have helped me more that anyone other than my mother. I have a plan, things are coming together. Thanks, you are a true brother in arms. Call me later."

I felt good. It was the same kind of feeling as when I took care of my small unit in Vietnam.

Gary died two hours later of a heart attack. The military funeral was tough—taps was played. I saluted my combat friend, who had become so close to me and whose years of struggles I understood.

Editors' note: George A. Hill is a disabled veteran and freelance writer. He has completed the VA Bay Pines, FL eight-week stress recovery unit (SRU) program and the Augusta, GA seven- and 14-week war trauma projects. He served one full and two partial (22 months) tours in Vietnam with the Marine Corps.

Ralph "Tripper" Sirianni
Sergeant, USMC, 2nd Bn 7th Reg,
Vietnam, 1969–1970

Vietnam taught me how to build defensive barriers to keep in the pain. I'm finally realizing this, after so many years. When I returned from my tour of duty I began a journey down another tunnel that was, in many ways, as dark as Nam. Although the element of fear so prevalent in Vietnam was not as obvious, I found myself caught in a world of denial, dangerous bouts of depression, failing health, and fantasy. I believe the denial and fantasy worked hand-in-hand. However, the main reason for my self-abusive behavior was a direct result of my combat experiences.

I lost touch with myself and that was fine, because in doing so I could dig a shallow grave for the past. As an artist it would've been so much more productive to paint what I was feeling, but instead my emotions were often expressed in violent rage or uncontrollable wailing. I couldn't love myself but I could "use" myself. I was the doctor and the patient—the scientist and the subject of the experiment. While I was using me, I had no problem using others.

Death took on a new meaning. If a person lived past 20 and died, my feelings were that at least they got to live that long, and their life wasn't brutally taken from them. Going to a wake . . . well, I've just lately begun attending occasionally. It's very unsettling for me to be in that environment.

Religion took a nose-dive that day a chopper brought a chaplain out to the bush for a church service. We had just lost some guys. He told us, in so many words, that we were "doing the right thing out here, fighting for our county," as he looked about nervously, blessed us, and was gone. It just didn't make sense. I never denounced God though, no matter how confused I got. He was always the one I asked for help when the shit got deep, kind of like a spiritual 911 call.

Nam was different for each individual there. Some guys, who never saw actual combat, came away with nightmares. The fear and ever-present threat of mutilation, death or being taken prisoner was so strong for many. Coping mechanisms were the weapons and tools of the trade. We didn't leave them behind upon our return home. Instead we found reinforcing components that were not always progressive. My coping tool turned out to be a shovel and I could only dig deeper.

I'd like to skip over a lot of that dark period and get to the present. I've been substance-free since June 12, 1992. Dealing with things with a clear mind is amazing. I've accomplished so much lately and I'm more confident about the future, although it won't be easy, but I have more patience to see things through now. Emotions are hard to mask. I can't come down on myself for shedding tears, I have to accept that. Exercise has played a very important part in keeping myself from falling totally over the edge. I do a considerable amount of running and lifting. That, coupled with a loving, supportive family and tight circle of friends, gave me something to live for. If others believe in you, eventually you come around to believing in yourself.

EPILOGUE

The editors found few stronger examples of the healing process than in a conversation with author Kellan Kyllo during the final stages of editing this book.

Soldier's Heart takes its form from veterans' writings. As we worked to organize the book, we noticed that Kellan's previously published work, *Where Light Is As Darkness*, contributed material to every chapter in *Soldier's Heart*—except the last. Kellan's poetry gives insight to many of the views of combat trauma, but it seemed that he had not resolved his problems with PTSD by 1991, when his book was published. Because it was necessary to contact Kellan to discuss using his copyrighted material, we explained the way *Soldier's Heart* was coming together, noting, "Your poetry is in every chapter, except . . ."

"Except the last!" he interrupted. "I hadn't worked through my problems at the time I wrote them."

". . . except the last," we agreed. "We wondered what happened to you, and think other vets who read your work will wonder as well."

"I'm retired and enjoying life," Kellan began, then discussed his success in college, as Farmer of the Year, and his problems with PTSD. He finished saying, "We lived an awful lot of years in the time we spent In Country. I've had a lot to catch up on, and haven't written about my experience in a long time. Don't know if I still have it in me to write about Vietnam."

A few days later he wrote the following poem, which is not only an appropriate conclusion to *Soldier's Heart*, but also to a veteran's return home from war.

Retirement

Kellan Kyllo
USMC, HMM-162, Ky Ha, Marble Mountain,
Quang Tri, Vietnam, 1966–1968

When the emotions
of war
finally started to slow down inside him
he
sold his guns,
and then soon after that he began
to forgive
all the people who had ever
done him
wrong,
and he prayed for each of them
daily.
The next Spring
he went into his backyard
for the first time
in twenty-five
years
and planted a garden.
He grew tomatoes and gave them away
to
everyone.

THEATER MAPS

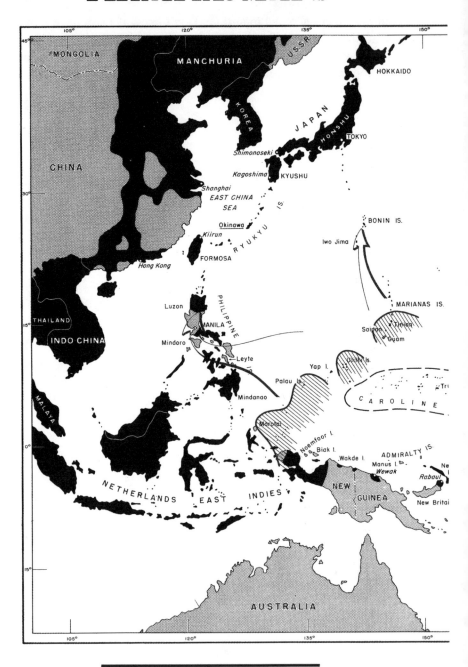

**Strategic Situation In The Pacific,
October 1944–March 1945**

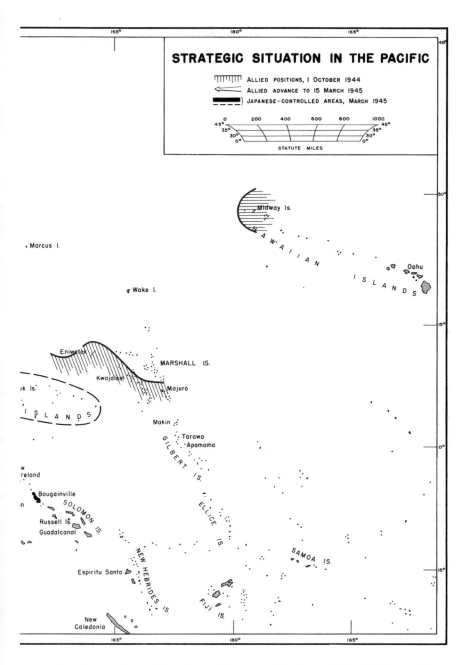

Appleman, Burns, Gugeler and Stevens, *U.S. Army in World War II: The War in the Pacific; Okinawa: The Last Battle*, (Center of Military History, United States Army, Washington, D.C., 1991)

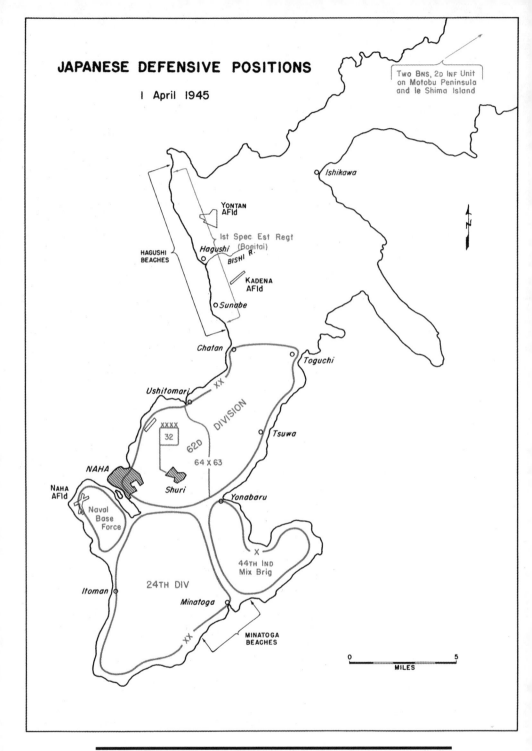

Japanese Defensive Positions on Okinawa, 1 April 1945

Appleman, Burns, Gugeler and Stevens, *U.S. Army in World War II: The War in the Pacific; Okinawa: The Last Battle*, (Center of Military History, United States Army, Washington, D.C., 1991)

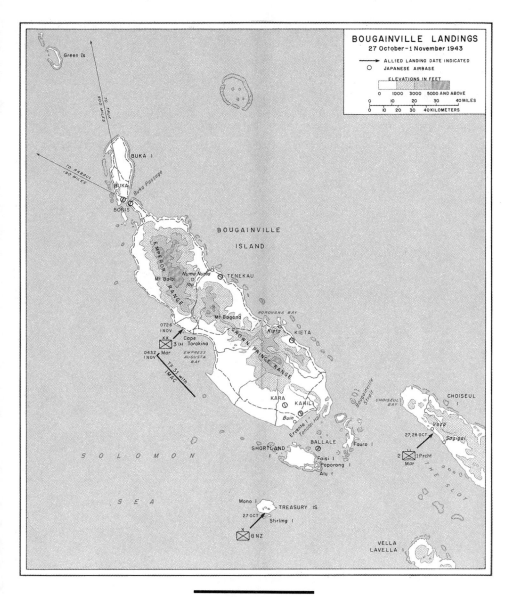

Bougainville Island

Miller, *U.S. Army in World War II: The War in the Pacific, Cartwheel: The Reduction of Rabaul*, (Center of Military History, United States Army, Washington, D.C., 1990)

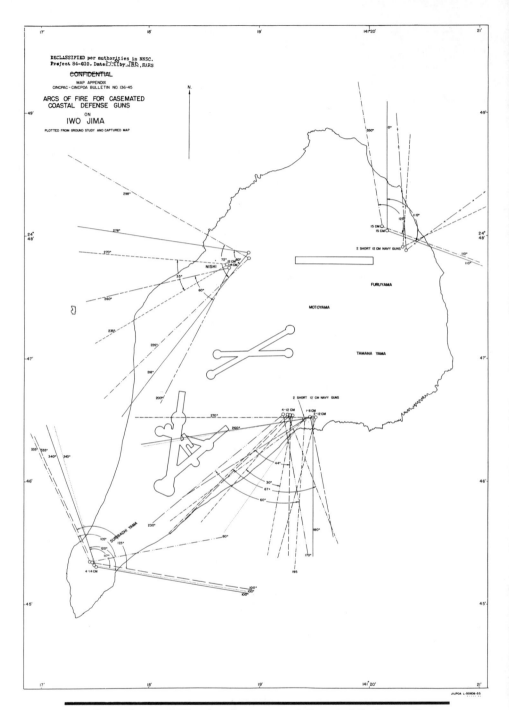

Iwo Jima: Arcs of Fire for Casemated Coastal Defense Guns, February 1945

Plotted from Captured Japanese Maps. National Archives Cartographic Reference Section.

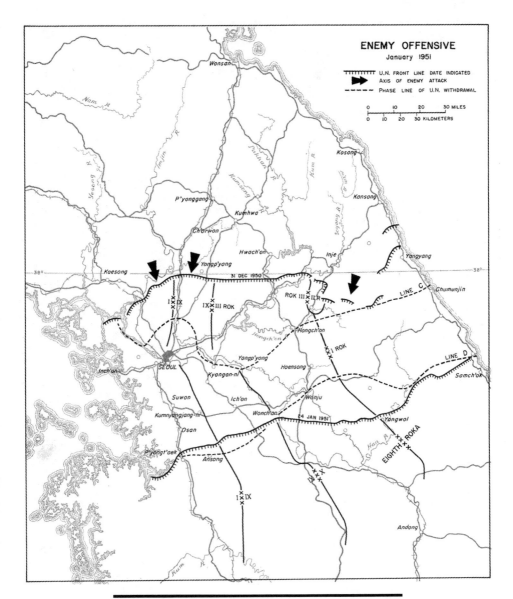

South Korea: Enemy Offensive, January 1951

Miller, Carroll, Tackley, *Korea: 1951-1953*, (Office of the Chief of Military History, Department of the Army, Washington, D.C., 1982) p 2.

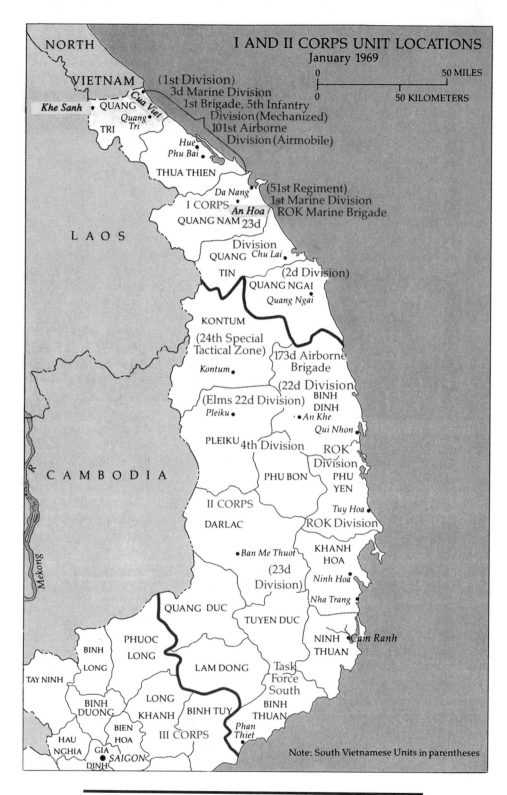

Vietnam: I and II Corps Unit Locations, January 1969

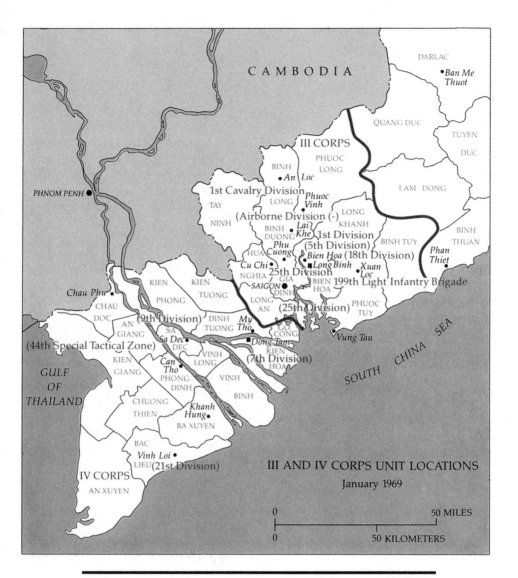

Vietnam: III and IV Corps Unit Locations, January 1969

Clarke, *Advice and Support: The Final Years: The U.S. Army in Vietnam.* (Center of Military History, United States Army, Washington, D.C., 1988) pp. 394 and 407.

MILITARY UNITS

A brief description of units identified by contributors follows.

UNITED STATES ARMY

DIVISION

Fourth Infantry Division (Ivy). Named for its roman numerals "IV." Served at the Argonne (W.W. I); Utah Beach, Heurtegen Forest, Ardennes (W.W. II); Central Highlands (II Corps) Vietnam, September 1966 to December 1970, (16,884 KIA/WIA).

Twenty Third Infantry Division (Americal). Originally formed from troops in place at New Caledonia, 1942. Reactivated in Vietnam, September 1967. Served principally in southern I Corps until disbanded in December 1971.

Twenty Fifth Infantry Division (Tropic Lightning). Initial combat on December 7, 1941. Subsequent W.W. II service at Guadalcanal and Luzon. Korea, 1950 to 1954. Vietnam, March 1966 to 1970. Stationed in III Corps, west and northwest of Saigon (34,484 KIA/WIA).

One Hundred First Airborne Division (Screaming Eagles). Initial combat W.W. II in Normandy, subsequent W.W. II operations: Operation Market-Garden, the siege of Bastogne, and the battle of the

Ruhr pocket. Arrived Vietnam, November 1967. Completely airmobile, divisional elements saw combat in all areas of that country with particular emphasis in the Central Highlands and the A Shau Valley (over 20,000 KIA/WIA). The last Army division to leave Vietnam (1972).

BRIGADE

One Hundred Seventy Third Airborne (Sky Soldiers), also known as the "Third Herd." Served in Vietnam, May 1965 to August 1971. Presidential Unit Citation at Battle of Dak To (November 1967).

BATTALION/REGIMENT

4th Bn 3rd Infantry (The Old Guard). Operated as part of 11th and 198th Brigades, Americal Division in southern I Corps, December 1967 to November 1971, at such sites as Duc Pho, Chu Lai, and Dong Ha.

2nd Bn 16th Infantry. Part of First Infantry Division in Vietnam, July 1965 to April 1970. Served in III Corps at Di An, Lai Khe, and Bien Hoa.

2nd Bn 7th Cavalry (Gary Owen). Airmobile infantry with First Cavalry Division. Served in Vietnam, September 1965 to May 1971. Participated in battle of Ia Drang Valley, October to November 1965.

5th Bn 7th Cavalry (Gary Owen). Airmobile Infantry with First Cavalry Division. Served in Vietnam, August 1966 to March 1971 at An Khe, Bien Hoa.

1st Bn 82nd Artillery. Supported Americal Units with 155 mm and 8 inch howitzer batteries. Based at Chu Lai, July 1968 to November 1971.

OTHER UNITS

75th Infantry (Merrill's Marauders). Provided Ranger Companies for Long Range Recon Patrols (LRRPs). Acted in support of all major USA units.

3rd Field Hospital. Established at Tan Son Nhut, April 1965. Formed US Army Saigon Hospital 1969. Departed Vietnam, May 1972.

336th Assault Helicopter Co. (Call signs: Warriors, T Birds). Vietnam, November 1966 to March 1971. Based at Soc Trang.

USA Security Service. Operated 8th Radio Research Field Station at Phu Bai, 1967 to 1968.

U.S. MARINE CORPS

DIVISION

First Marine Division, organized 1941. Served at Guadalcanal and Okinawa (W.W. II). Pusan Perimeter, Inchon, and the Chosin Reservoir (Korea). Vietnam, 1966 to 1971 with responsibility for southern I Corps. Awarded two Presidential Unit citations (Battle of Hue City, 1968).

Third Marine Division, organized 1942. Served at Bougainville, Guam, and Iwo Jima (W.W. II). Arrived Vietnam, March 1965. Ultimately assumed responsibility for northern I Corps and the Demilitarized Zone (DMZ). Awarded Presidential Unit Citation for the Khe Sanh hill battles (881N, 881S, 861). Held Khe Sanh against NVA forces during the 1968 siege. Departed Vietnam, 1969, returned for evacuation of Saigon and Mayaguez rescue.

BATTALION/REGIMENT

2nd Bn 1st Regiment. Primarily active in southern I Corps. For further information re 1968 to 1969, see *Fortunate Son* by Lewis Puller, Jr.

2nd Bn 3rd Regiment (Widowmakers). Often employed as part
of a Special Landing Force (SLF). Awarded Presidential Unit Citation
for its role in the "hill fights" (Khe Sanh, 1967).

3rd Bn 5th Regiment. Served in Vietnam, May 1966 to March 1971.
Operated from An Hoa in 1969 and patrolled a highly contested area
called the "Arizona territory."

2nd Bn 7th Regiment. Served in Vietnam, August 1965 to October
1970. Primary area of activity was southern I Corps.

Battery F 2nd Bn 11th Regiment. Artillery in support of First Division
units. Battery F usually fired for 5th and 7th Marines.

MARINE AVIATION

First Marine Air Wing (1st MAW). In Vietnam, controlled up to six
Marine Air Groups (MAG): three fixed wing Groups flying F4s, A4s,
and A6s from Da Nang and Chu Lai; three Groups flying UH-34,
CH-46, CH-53, and UH-1E helicopters from Da Nang, Chu Lai,
Quang Tri, and Phu Bai. In five years of Vietnam service, 1st MAW
lost 252 helicopters and 173 fixed wing aircraft to combat action.

HMM-162, Marine Medium Helicopter squadron. Arrived Da Nang,
March 1965 flying UH-34s, often deployed with the Special Landing
Force.

HMM-362 (The Ugly Angels). Marine Medium Helicopter squadron.
First Marine helicopter squadron in Vietnam. UH-34D aircraft arrived
Soc Trang, April 1962, identified many of the problems surrounding
helicopter operations and developed operational tactics. Last squadron
to fly UH-34 aircraft in Vietnam, August 1969.

US NAVY

Task Force 116 (River Patrol Force). Established Vietnam, December
1965 to deny VC and NVA the use of waterways for resupply. Initially
employed 28 foot fiberglass patrol boats (PBRs), later replaced by
aluminum craft.

RESOURCES

The resources listed here are intended to give people a starting place for their own exploration into the programs and organizations available to veterans with PTSD and their families.

Organizations

Listed here are the national headquarters of these organizations, which operate support groups in every state. You may contact them to find the branch or chapter nearest you.

Alcoholics Anonymous
General Service Office
P. O. Box 459
Grand Central Station
New York, NY 10163
(212) 870-3400

Al-Anon, Alateen
Family Group Headquarters
P.O. Box 862
Midtown Station
New York, NY 10018-0862
(800) 356-9996

Narcotics Anonymous
P.O. Box 9999
Van Nuys, CA 91409
(818) 780-3951

Nar-Anon
World Service Office
P.O. Box 2562
Palos Verdes, CA 90274
(213) 547-5800

Parents Anonymous
(child abuse)
675 W. Foothill Blvd., Suite 220
Claremont, CA 91711
(909) 621-6184

Disabled American Veterans
807 Maine Avenue, S.W.
Washington, D.C. 20024
(202) 554-3501

Vietnam Veterans of America
1224 M Street, N.W.
Washington, D.C. 20005
(202) 628-2700

Department of Veterans Affairs
(for information about PTSD
treatment at your closest V.A.
hospital)
810 Vermont Avenue, N.W.
Washington, D.C. 20420
(202) 273-5400

Veterans Outreach Centers

Anchorage, AK 99508   4201 Tudor Centre Dr., Suite 115

Fairbanks, AK 99701   520 5th Ave., Suite 104

Kenai, AK 99611   P.O. Box 1883

Wasilla, AK 99654   851 E. Westpoint Ave., Suite 109

Birmingham, AL 35205   1425 S. 21st St., Suite 108

Mobile, AL 36604   951 Government St., Suite 122

North Little Rock, AR 72114   201 W. Broadway, Suite A

Phoenix, AZ 85004   141 E. Palm Ln., Suite 100

Prescott, AZ 86301   637 Hillside Ave., Suite A

Tuscon, AZ 85719   3055 N. 1st Ave.

Anaheim, CA 92805   859 S. Harbor Blvd.

Benicia, CA 94510   555 1st St., Suite 200

Burlingame, CA 94010   1234 Howard — San Mateo

Chico, CA 95926   109 Parmac Rd.

Commerce, CA 90040   5400 E. Olympic Blvd., #140

Concord, CA 94520   1899 Clayton Rd., Suite 140

Eureka, CA 95501   305 V St.

Fresno, CA 93726   3636 N. 1st St., Suite 112

Los Angeles, CA 90003   251 W. 85th Pl.

Los Angeles, CA 90025   2000 Westwood Blvd.

Marina, CA 93933   455 Reservation Rd., Suite E

Oakland, CA 94612   287 17th St.

Riverside, CA 92504   4954 Arlington Ave., Suite A

Rohnert Park, CA 94928   6225 State Farm Dr., Suite 101

Sacramento, CA 95825   1111 Howe Ave., Suite 390

San Diego, CA 92103   2900 6th Ave.

San Francisco, CA 94102   25 Van Ness Ave.

San Jose, CA 95112   278 N. 2nd St.

Santa Barbara, CA 93101   1300 Santa Barbara St.

Sepulveda, CA 91343   16126 Lassen St.

Upland, CA 91786   313 N. Mountain Ave.

Vista, CA 92083   1830 West Dr., Suite 103

Boulder, CO 80302   2128 Pearl St.

Colorado Springs, CO 80903   411 S. Tejon, Suite G

Denver, CO 80204   1815 Federal Blvd.

Hartford, CT 06120   370 Market St.

Norwich, CT 06360   100 Main St.

West Haven, CT 06516   141 Capt. Thomas Blvd.

Washington, D.C. 20003   801 Pennsylvania Ave., S.E.

Wilmington, DE 19805   1601 Kirkwood Hwy., VAMROC Bldg 2

Fort Lauderdale, FL 33301   315 N.E. 3rd Ave.

Jacksonville, FL 32202   255 Liberty St.

Lake Worth, FL 33461   2311 10th Ave., North #13 Palm Beach

Miami, FL 33129   2700 S.W. 3rd Ave., Suite 1A

Orlando, FL 32809   5001 S. Orange Ave., Suite A

Pensacola, FL 32501   202 W. Jackson

Sarasota, FL 34239   1800 Siesta Dr.

St. Petersburg, FL 33713   2837 1st Ave., N.

Tallahassee, FL 32303   249 E. 6th Ave.

Tampa, FL 33604   1507 W. Sligh Ave.

Atlanta, GA 30309   922 W. Peachtree St.

Savannah, GA 31406   8110 A White Bluff Rd.

Hilo, HI 96720   120 Keawe St., Suite 201

Honolulu, HI 96814   1680 Kapiolani Blvd., Suite F

Kailua-Kona, HI 96740   75-5995 Kuakini Hwy., #415

Lihue, HI 96766   3367 Kuhio Hwy., Suite 101-Kauai

Wailuku, HI 96793   Ting Bldg., 35 Lunalilo, Suite 101

Des Moines, IA 50310   2600 Harding Rd.

Sioux City, IA 51105   706 Jackson

Boise, ID 83706   1115 W. Boise Ave.

Pocatello, ID 83201   1975 S. 5th St.

Chicago, IL 60637   5505 S. Harper

Chicago Heights, IL 60411   1600 Halsted St.

East St. Louis, IL 62203   1269 N. 89th St., Suite 1

Evanston, IL 60202   565 Howard St.

Moline, IL 61265   1529 46th Ave., Room 6

Oak Park, IL 60302   155 S. Oak Park Ave.

Peoria, IL 61603   605 N.E. Monroe St.

Springfield, IL 62703   624 S. 4th St.

Evansville, IN 47711   311 N. Weinbach Ave.

Fort Wayne, IN 46802   528 West Berry St.

Gary, IN 46408   2236 West Ridge Rd.

Indianapolis, IN 46208   3833 N. Meridian, Suite 120

Wichita, KS 67211   413 S. Pattie

Lexington, KY 40503   1117 Limestone Rd.

Louisville, KY 40208   1355 S. 3rd St.

Bossier City, LA 71112   2103 Old Minden Rd.

New Orleans, LA 70116   1529 N. Claiborne Ave.

Shreveport, LA 71104   2620 Centenary Blvd., Bldg. 3, Suite 260

Boston, MA 02215   665 Beacon St.

Brockton, MA 02401   1041 L Pearl St.

Lawrence, MA 01840   45 Franklin St.

Lowell, MA 01852   73 East Merrimack St.

New Bedford, MA 02740   468 North St.

Springfield, MA 01103   1985 Main St., Northgate Plaza

Winchendon, MA 01475   Town Hall

Worcester, MA 01605   108 Grove St.

Baltimore, MD 21230   777 Washington Blvd.

Cambridge, MD 21613   5510 W. Shore Dr.

Elkton, MD 21921   7 Elkton Commercial Plaza, S. Bridge St.

Silver Spring, MD 20910   1015 Spring St., Suite 101

Bangor, ME 04401   352 Harlow St.

Caribou, ME 04736   228 Sweden St.

Lewiston, ME 04240   475 Pleasant St.

Portland, ME 04101   63 Preble St.

Sanford, ME 04073   441 Main St.

Grand Rapids, MI 49507   1940 Eastern Ave. S.E.

Lincoln Park, MI 48146   1766 Fort St.

Oak Park, MI 48237   20820 Greenfield Rd.

Duluth, MN 55802   405 E. Superior St.

St. Paul, MN 55114   2480 University Ave.

Kansas City, MO 64111   3931 Main St.

St. Louis, MO 63103   2345 Pine St.

Biloxi, MS 39531   2196 Pass Rd.

Jackson, MS 39206   4436 N. State St., Suite A3

Billings, MT 59102   1948 Grand Ave.

Missoula, MT 59802   500 N. Higgins Ave.

Charlotte, NC 28202   223 S. Brevard St., Suite 103

Fayetteville, NC 28301   4 Market Square

Greensboro, NC 27406   2009 Elm-Eugene St.

Greenville, NC 27834   150 Arlington Blvd., Suite B

Fargo, ND 58103   1322 Gateway Dr.

Minot, ND 58702   2041 3rd St. N.W.

Lincoln, NE 68508   920 L St.

Omaha, NE 68106   5123 Leavenworth St.

Manchester, NH 03104   103 Liberty St.

Jersey City, NJ 07302   115 Christopher Columbus Dr., Rm. 200

Linwood, NJ 08221   222 New Rd., Bldg. 2, Suite 405

Newark, NJ 07102   77 Halsey St.

Trenton, NJ 08611   171 Jersey St., Bldg. 36

Albuquerque, NM 87104   1600 Mountain Rd., N.W.

Farmington, NM 87402   4251 E. Main, Suite B

Santa Fe, NM 87505   1996 Warner St., Warner Plaza, Suite 5

Las Vegas, NV 89101   704 S. 6th St.

Reno, NV 89503   1155 W. 4th St., Suite 101

Albany, NY 12206   875 Central Ave.

Babylon, NY 11702   116 West Main St.

Bronx, NY 10458   226 East Fordham Rd., Rms. 216-217

Brooklyn, NY 11201   165 Cadman Plaza East

Buffalo, NY 14209   351 Linwood Ave.

New York, NY 10036   120 West 44th St., Suite 201

New York, NY 10027   55 W. 125th St.

Rochester, NY 14608   134 S. Fitzhugh St.

Staten Island, NY 10301   150 Richmond Terr.

Syracuse, NY 13203   210 North Townsend St.

White Plains, NY 10601   200 Hamilton Ave., White Plains Mall

Woodhaven, NY 11421   75-1OB 91st Ave.

Cincinnati, OH 45219   30 E. Hollister St.

Cleveland, OH 44111   11511 Lorain Ave.

Cleveland Heights, OH 44118   2134 Lee Rd.

Columbus, OH 43205   1054 E. Broad St.

Dayton, OH 45402   6 S. Patterson Blvd.

Oklahoma City, OK 73105   3033 N. Walnut, Suite 101W

Tulsa, OK 74101   1855 E. 15th St.

Eugene, OR 97403   1966 Garden Ave.

Grants Pass, OR 97526-3214   211 S.E. 10th St.

Portland, OR 97220   8383 N.E. Sandy Blvd., Suite 110

Salem, OR 97301   318 Church St., N.E.

Erie, PA 16501   G. Daniel Baldwin Bldg., 1000 State St.

Harrisburg, PA 17110   1007 N. Front St.

McKeesport, PA 15132   500 Walnut St.

Philadelphia, PA 19107   1026 Arch St.

Philadelphia, PA 19120   101 E. Olney Ave., Box C-7

Pittsburgh, PA 15222   954 Penn Ave.

Scranton, PA 18509   959 Wyoming Ave.

Arecibo, Puerto Rico 00612   52 Gonzalo Marin St.

Ponce, Puerto Rico 00731   35 Mayor St.

Rio Pedras, Puerto Rico 00921   Suite LC8A & LC9, La Riviera

Cranston, R.I. 02920   789 Park Ave.

Columbia, S.C. 29201   1313 Elmwood Ave.

Greenville, S.C. 29601   904 Pendleton St.

North Charleston, S.C. 29406   5603A Rivers Ave.

Rapid City, SD 57701   610 Kansas City St.

Sioux Falls, SD 57104   601 S. Cliff Ave., Suite C

Chattanooga, TN 37404   425 Cumberland St., Suite 140

Johnson City, TN 37601   703 S. Roan St.

Knoxville, TN 37914   2817 E. Magnolia Ave.

Memphis, TN 38104   1835 Union, Suite 100

Amarillo, TX 79106   3414 E. Olsen Blvd., Suite E

Austin, TX 78723   3401 Manor Rd., Suite 102

Corpus Christi, TX 78404   3166 Reid Dr., Suite 1

Dallas, TX 75244   5232 Forest Ln., Suite 111

El Paso, TX 79924   6500 Boeing, Suite L112

Fort Worth, TX 76104   1305 W. Magnolia, Suite B

Houston, TX 77004   4905A San Jacinto

Houston, TX 77007   8100 Washington Ave., Suite 120

Laredo, TX 78041   6020 McPherson Rd., #1

Lubbock, TX 79410   3208 34th St.

McAllen, TX 78501   1317 E. Hackberry St.

Midland, TX 79703   3404 W. Illinois, Suite 1

San Antonio, TX 78212   231 W. Cypress St.

Provo, UT 84601   750 North 200 West, Suite 105

Salt Lake City, UT 84106   1354 East 3300 South

Norfolk, VA 23517   2200 Colonial Ave., Suite 3

Richmond, VA 23230   3022 W. Clay St.

Roanoke, VA 24016   320 Mountain Ave., S.W.

Springfield, VA 22150   7024 Spring Garden Dr., Brookfield Plaza

St. Croix, Virgin Islands 00820   Village Mall, Barren Spot

St. Thomas, Virgin Islands 00801   Upper Havensight Mall

South Burlington, VT 05403   359 Dorset St.

White River Junction, VT 05001   Gilman Office Center, Bldg. 2, Holiday Inn Dr.

Seattle, WA 98121   2230 8th Ave.

Spokane, WA 99201   1708 W. Mission St.

Tacoma, WA 98409   4916 Center St., Suite E

Madison, WI 53703   147 S. Butler St.

Milwaukee, WI 53208   3400 Wisconsin

Beckley, WV 25801   101 Ellison Ave.

Charleston, WV 25312   512 Washington St. West

Huntington, WV 25701   1005 6th Ave.

Martinsburg, WV 25401   105 S. Spring St.

Morgantown, WV 26505   1191 Pineview Dr.

Princeton, WV 24740   905 Mercer St.

Wheeling, WV 26003   1070 Market St.

Casper, WY 82601   111 S. Jefferson, Suite 100

Cheyenne, WY 82001   3130 Henderson Dr.

Publications of Related Interest

Please note that some of these books may be out of print and no longer available for purchase. However, such books may be available at libraries.

About PTSD

Bourne, Peter G., M.D. *Men, Stress and Vietnam.* (Boston, MA: Little Brown & Co., 1970) How the predetermined one-year tour affected American soldiers. For all readers.

Goodwin, J. Psy. D. *Continuing Readjustment Problems Among Vietnam Veterans.* (Ohio: Disabled American Veterans, 1980 Pamphlet) A description of Post Traumatic Stress Disorder, its evolution, and symptoms in the Vietnam veteran. This easily understood pamphlet describes the major symptoms of PTSD in a way that's recognizable to the veteran and his or her family. It covers: The Evolution of PTSD; How the Vietnam Experience Differed from Previous Wars; Catalysts of PTSD; Symptoms (Depression, Isolation, Rage, Alienation, Survival Guilt, Anxiety, Nightmares, and Intrusive/Obsessive Thoughts). The pamphlet concludes with an overview of treatment options. For all readers.

Figley, Charles R. (ed.) *Stress Disorders Among Vietnam Veterans.* (New York: Brunner/Mazel, 1978) Edited by a Marine combat veteran, this collection is a primary source on treatment issues. For clinicians.

Herman, Judith. *Trauma and Recovery.* (New York: Basic Books, 1992) A theoretical synthesis of how survivors are affected by trauma. Drawing from the experience of people who survived the holocaust, combat trauma, rape, child abuse, domestic violence, and torture as prisoners of war or political prisoners, Herman explains the symptoms and enduring personality changes that result from trauma and how the symptoms are related to the trauma. She clarifies the process of healing in a very readable analysis. All readers.

Kulka, Richard, et al. *Trauma and the Vietnam War Generation.* (New York: Brunner/Mazel, 1990) The report to Congress on the findings of the National Vietnam Veterans Readjustment Study. For clinicians.

Chapter 1. Something's Wrong

Baker, Mark. *Nam: The Vietnam War in the Words of the Men and Women Who Fought There.* (New York: Morrow, 1982) Oral history memoirs of 100 men and women who served in Vietnam. All readers.

Caputo, Philip. *A Rumor of War*. (New York: Ballantine Books, 1977) Caputo, who won the Pulitzer Prize in 1972 for coverage of primary election fraud, was an infantry officer with the 9th Marine Expeditionary Brigade, the first combat unit sent to Vietnam in 1965. Based on his 16-month tour in I Corps (Da Nang, Hue-Phu Bai), Caputo's autobiographical account brings to life the range of extreme, conflicting emotions felt by combatants—emotions which were the first seeds of PTSD. *"Anyone who fought in Vietnam, if he is honest about himself, will have to admit he enjoyed the compelling attractiveness of combat. It was a peculiar enjoyment because it was mixed with commensurate pain. . . . it made whatever else life offered in the way of delights or torments seem pedestrian."* All readers.

Freedman, D. & Rhoads, J. *Nurses in Vietnam: The Forgotten Veterans*. (Austin, TX: Texas Monthly Press, Inc., 1987) The oral history of nine nurses who served in Vietnam. These women recount their war experiences and the impact on their lives. The work describes the efforts of some to seek help for PTSD. Highlights the common elements of the war experience and PTSD for both combatants and nurses. All readers, particularly women veterans.

Goldman, P. & Fuller, T. *Charlie Company: What Vietnam Did to Us*. (New York: William Morrow & Co., 1983) Charlie Co. reunites after the war. All readers.

Kyllo, Kellan. *Where Light Is As Darkness*. (Minneapolis, MN: New Sweden Press, 1991) Written before the author himself came to terms with his PTSD, Kyllo's poetry spans the course of the disorder, capturing sights, sounds, and feelings familiar to every afflicted veteran. A sensitive and thought-provoking work to help a vet put difficult feelings into words and generate discussion with spouse and family. All readers.

Leckie, Robert. *Helmet for My Pillow*. An autobiographical account of combat service with the U.S. Marine Corps' Pacific campaign during W. W. II. Well written, it provides a grunt's perspective. All readers.

Russ, Martin. *The Last Parallel*. (New York: Rinehart & Co., 1957) An auto-biographical account of combat during the latter portion of the Korean War. All readers.

Puller, Lewis B. Jr., *Fortunate Son*. (New York: Bantam Books, 1993) Awarded the Pulitzer Prize, this autobiography follows Puller, son of Marine legend "Chesty" Puller, from his early life with his famous father on posts of the Corps, to the moment a Viet Cong booby-trap amputated his legs, to homecoming and his struggle to deal with his devastating wounds and alcoholism. Bred to idealism, Puller displays the frustration of many vets who have given the last measure of devotion, yet feel compelled to bottle their anger. All readers.

Santoli, Al. *Everything We Had: An Oral History of the Vietnam War.* (New York: Random House, 1981) Santoli, a decorated rifleman with the 25th Infantry Division, opens chronological "windows" on the Vietnam experience through the personal accounts of 33 American men and women. Beginning with recollections of the nine-to-five war under Kennedy in 1962, *Everything We Had* travels through free kill zones, POW camps and hospital wards, and ends with the fall of Saigon in 1975. The recollections of combat and personal tragedy are graphic and compelling, and at times give the reader the uncomfortable sense of eavesdropping on unguarded feelings. All readers.

Terry, W. *Bloods: An Oral History of the Vietnam War by Black Veterans.* (New York: Random House, 1984) Terry, a journalist who covered the Vietnam War for two years for "Time" magazine outlines the complex and unique experience of the African-American soldiers. He develops a portrait of the experience through interviews with 20 soldiers who have their own stories to share. The African-American soldier fought in Vietnam during one of the most tumultuous socio-political eras in this century. As the Civil Rights Movement and the Black Nationalist Movement gained momentum in the United States, African-American soldiers accounted for more than 23 percent of fatalities in Vietnam. *Bloods* provides the clinician and general reader an overview of the relationship between these world events, soldiers' experience and their subsequent readjustment.

Webb, James. *Fields of Fire.* (New Jersey: Prentice Hall, 1978) James Webb, the first Naval Academy graduate to become the Secretary of the Navy, won the Navy Cross, Silver Star, two Bronze Stars and a Purple Heart as a Marine officer in Vietnam in 1969. *Fields of Fire* follows a platoon of young Marines through the tropical heat of the An Hoa Basin, "out in the boonies" southwest of Da Nang. Webb's Marines complain bitterly of their hardships, yet many re-enlist because war has come to be the game they play best, and ultimately the only reality they know. Yet, coming home, a young survivor questions, *"The only meaning was the thing itself. And what does it get me to know that?"* All readers.

Chapter 2. Isolation

Greene, Bob. *Home-coming: When the Soldiers Returned From Vietnam.* (New York: G. P. Putnam's Sons, 1989) A syndicated columnist for the Chicago "Tribune," Greene put a question to his readers who were Vietnam veterans: "Were you ever spat upon when you returned to the United States?" Their responses capture the emotional impact of returning to America from Vietnam and cover a wide range of feelings. This book provides a firsthand view of the society veterans came home to after their service. All readers.

Chapter 3. Seeking Help

Figley, Charles R. and Leventman, S. (eds.) *Strangers at Home: Vietnam Veterans Since the War.* (New York: Praeger, 1980) The thrust of this collection is to give a social/political/psychological perspective to the war and to delineate problems of the Vietnam veteran today. For clinicians.

Manchester, William. *Goodbye Darkness.* (Boston, MA: Little, Brown, 1980) Manchester entered W. W. II as a Marine infantryman near the end of the battle for Guadalcanal (1942), as the fighting on that island concluded. His own combat experience was on Okinawa in 1945, where he was seriously wounded after two months of intense combat. The author became plagued with a recurring nightmare some time after the war, after throwing a war memento into a river. The nightmares took form as recurrent dreams of the author as a young Sergeant, taking his older self to task for surviving, and questioning the use he had made of the world. Manchester travels to the major battlefields of the Pacific to vanquish his ghost. The work ends reflecting on the values and strengths of pre-W.W. II society, which Manchester sees as enabling his generation to have fought and won the war, and ends stating, "Later the rules would change. But we didn't know that then. We didn't *know.*" All readers.

Matsakis, Aphrodite. *I Can't Get Over It: A Handbook for Trauma Survivors.* (Oakland: New Harbinger Publications, Inc., 1992) A step-by-step guide to understanding trauma as a normal reaction to abnormal stress. The book defines PTSD, and explains some of the physical and psychological changes that accompany traumatic stress. Many exercises are provided to increase understanding and coping skills, as well as clear information on why the process of healing is important and how it works. Several chapters are devoted to specific kinds of trauma, from combat to car accidents. All readers.

Van Devanter, Linda M. *Home Before Morning: The Story of an Army Nurse in Vietnam.* (New York: Beaufort Books, 1983) This autobiographical account follows the author's experience from her nurse's training, through her year in operating rooms in Vietnam, to the readjustment problems she experienced on homecoming, and the resolution to her problems that she achieved. The book provides insight into the unique challenges faced by female veterans: their concerns about the validity of their PTSD symptoms; feeling alone in a world of men; concern about the effect of Agent Orange on the endocrine system and reproductive health. The book outlines the author's attempts to find help for combat-related PTSD, as well as her process of healing. All readers.

Williams, Thomas, (ed.) *Post Traumatic Stress Disorders of the Vietnam Veteran.* (Ohio: Disabled American Veterans, 1980) Observations and recommendations for the psychological treatment of the veteran and his family. For clinicians.

Chapter 4. Despair

Kovic, Ron. *Born of the Fourth of July*. (New York: McGraw-Hill, 1976) An angry memoir by a Marine Sergeant who was paralyzed in the war, Kovic's story reveals the polarization Vietnam caused in American society and his despair as a disabled vet who no longer "fits in" with family or community. Protesting the war in which he was decorated, Kovic's medals were ripped from his chest by vets and non-vets who called him "traitor" at an anti-war rally. Nevertheless, Kovic finds a different kind of "togetherness" from what he knew in Vietnam, and becomes an activist with the Vietnam Veterans Against the War in order to heal himself and others. All readers.

Walker, K. *A Piece of My Heart: The Stories of Twenty-Six American Women Who Served in Vietnam*. (Novato, CA: Presidio Press, 1985) The narrators discuss their motivations for going to Vietnam, how the experience changed their lives, and for some, their difficulties dealing with PTSD. The women also question the possible link between Agent Orange exposure and current health problems for them and their children. The book acknowledges involvement in the Vietnam War of American women in non-military and non-nursing capacities. For all readers; of particular interest to women.

Chapter 5. Loss, Mourning, Grieving

Scruggs, J.C. & Swerdlow, J.L. *To Heal A Nation: The Vietnam Veterans Memorial*. (New York: Harper & Row, 1985) An account of the development of the Vietnam Veterans Memorial. This book gives an excellent description of the political and social climate of the times. All readers.

Chapter 6. Escape

Daley, Dennis, Moss, H., Campbell, F., *Dual Disorders: Counseling Clients With Chemical Dependency and Mental Illness*. (Center City, Minnesota, Hazelden Foundation, 1987) Divided into chapters on specific psychiatric disorders in conjunction with alcoholism, the book addresses issues specific to PTSD and alcoholism. For clinicians and general readers.

Gottheil, E., Druley, K., Pashko, S., Weinstein, S., *Stress and Addiction*. (New York, Brunner/Mazel, 1987) One of the psychosocial stress book series, addressed to clinicians, that covers alcohol and addiction with reference to PTSD.

Kane, Rod. *Veteran's Day*. (New York, Orion Books, 1990) Kane provides an open account of his experiences as a very young person going to war, and a clear description of his confusion upon returning home. A combat medic, the author uses his autobiographical sketch to detail intrusive memories, nightmares, problems with rage and relationships. He gives the reader a graphic description of his use of alcohol and drugs to numb his feelings and distance himself from others. Examples of his geographical wandering and adaptation to an isolated way of life further illustrate the author's attempt to cope with his PTSD symptoms. Throughout the recollection of his ordeal, he continues to "search for meaning in the experience," and emphasizes his need "to make sense of it all." Treatment references are somewhat dated, but clinicians and veterans can gain insight into the process of Post Traumatic Stress Disorder as well as potential treatment options. All readers.

Chapter 7. Families and Other Perspectives

Lopes, S. *The Wall.* (New York: Collins, 1987) Moving photographic album of veterans, families at the Vietnam Veterans Memorial. All readers.

Mason, Patience H.C. *Recovering From The War: A Woman's Guide to Helping Your Vietnam Vet, Your Family, and Yourself.* (New York, NY: Penguin Books, 1990) A survivor who has lived with her spouse's PTSD for over 20 years, Patience Mason introduces her book as intended "for women who have relationships with Vietnam veterans." Nevertheless, Mason's plain-language explanation of PTSD, and how vets and spouses can help themselves is particularly useful in showing the effect the vet has on his or her family. Many vets "can't speak about the war." Many spouses "don't like hearing about 'that scary stuff.' " Mason includes interviews with combat veterans as well as coping and treatment experiences to provide an excellent tool for generating conversation between husband and wife. All readers.

Matsakis, Aphrodite. *Vietnam Wives: Women and Children Surviving Life with Veterans Suffering Post Traumatic Stress Disorder, Second Edition.* (Lutherville, MD: Sidran Press, Forthcoming Spring 1996) A classic description of combat PTSD for the "significant other" who can't understand "why he acts that way." All readers.

Palmer, Laura, *Shrapnel in the Heart: Letters and Remembrances from the Vietnam Veterans Memorial.* (New York: Random House, 1987) An excellent and moving account of families and the loved ones whom they lost in the Vietnam War. All readers.

Chapter 8. Making Sense Of It All

Brende, J.O. & Parson, E.R. *Vietnam Veterans: The Road to Recovery.* New York: Plenum Press, 1985.

Egendorf, A. *Healing from the War: Trauma and Transformation After Vietnam.* (Boston: Houghton Mifflin Co., 1985) Written by a psychologist who coordinated "rap groups" in New York in the early 1970s this book is an exploration of healing, specifically around the Vietnam War, directed to the individual veteran and the country as a whole. More philosophical than theoretical, this is an attempt to create a bridge between those who supported the war, and those who opposed it, thereby providing help to all who were touched by Vietnam. All readers.

MacPherson, M. *Long Time Passing: Vietnam and the Haunted Generation.* (Garden City, NJ: Doubleday, 1984) A narrative that uses many interviews to illustrate veterans' experience with PTSD, Vet Centers, Canadian exile, war, and recovery, etc. All readers.

Zaczek, Ronald J. *Farewell Darkness: A Veteran's Triumph Over Combat Trauma.* (Annapolis, MD, The Naval Institute Press, 1994) A probing, personal look at war's psychological toll, the book spans the author's six years in treatment for PTSD in the Veterans Outreach Program. Recommended for veterans by Vietnam Veterans Memorial Fund president Jan Scruggs, Medal of Honor recipient Senator Bob Kerrey, and American Legion Executive Director John Sommer. PTSD researcher Dr. Charles Figley calls it an *"in your face narrative of (Zaczek's) years of recovery—just what vets and their families require to appreciate the tracks of trauma."* All readers.

GLOSSARY

12-Step Group   A group modeled on the Alcoholics Anonymous philosophy, which teaches that there are twelve steps to sobriety.

ADL   Activities of daily living, a term used in clinical settings to refer to activities such as personal hygiene, housekeeping, using public transportation, etc.

Agent Orange   A 50-50 mixture of 2,4-D and 2,4,5-T sprayed from aircraft and used to defoliate jungle areas in Vietnam; the name is derived from the orange-banded drums in which it was shipped. U.S. chemical companies which produced the chemical were the target of a class-action suit by Vietnam veterans who suffer, or whose children suffer, severe health problems they attribute to exposure to this toxic chemical.

AK47   Russian-made Kalashnikov, gas-operated 7.62 mm automatic assault rifle; 30 round banana-shaped magazine, range 400 meters. Standard weapon of the North Vietnamese and Viet Cong.

Arizona Territory   Triangle of fertile land and hamlets west, southwest of Da Nang, between the Vu Gia and Thu Bon rivers in which the 5th Marine Regiment saw heavy fighting in 1969.

ARVN   Army of the Republic of (South) Vietnam, also used to refer to an individual South Vietnamese soldier.

Auschwitz   Near Oswiecim in southwest Poland, site of the extermination of 4 million victims, mostly Jews, by the Germans in World War II.

Berkeley   The campus of the University of California at Berkeley, and other colleges and universities through the country, witnessed many student anti-Vietnam war demonstrations.

body bag   Olive-drab, rubberized sack that could be zipped tightly shut to transport human remains.

bush   Usually refers to the jungle, sometimes used for any area of jungle, rice paddies, or tall grass where armed patrols search for the enemy.

Cambodia   Borders South Vietnam on the west, used as a staging area for enemy operations during the Vietnam War.

Chloral Hydrate   A sedative.

Chu Lai   A main American airbase in Quang Tin Province, South Vietnam (southern I Corps.)

claim   A petition filed by a veteran to receive disability income from the Department of Veterans Affairs for a service-connected injury.

Clark Field (Philippine Islands)   One of several processing centers for troops returning home from Vietnam.

COSVN   Central Office of South Vietnam, the nominal Communist military and political headquarters in South Vietnam.

CP   Command Post.

crepitation of pneumothorax   The crackling sound made by air entering the chest cavity through a perforation in the chest wall.

Cua Viet   River just south of the Vietnamese Demilitarized Zone in Quang Tri Province. Site of Marine amphibious landings.

DEROS   Date of Estimated (or Expected) Return from Overseas. The tour of duty for most U.S. servicemen in Vietnam was 12 months. Marines, noted for one-upsmanship, served 13 months.

Devils' Island   French penal colony off the coast of Guyana in South America noted for its harsh living conditions, cruelty, and being virtually "escape-proof" due to its snake-infested jungle.

Domino Theory   Theory put forth by the U.S. government to justify America's involvement in Vietnam, that if Vietnam fell to Communist rule, so too would neighboring Asian nations.

door gunner   Armed helicopters, (e.g., CH-46 Sea Knight, CH-47 Chinook, UH-34 Iroquois, UH-1E Huey and CH-53 Sea Stallion) were crewed by a pilot, copilot, crewchief, and gunner. During combat missions, UH-34, CH-53 and Huey crewchiefs and gunners fired 7.62 mm M-60 machine guns mounted in the aircraft doors; -46 and -47 crews manned .50 caliber weapons.

DVA   Department of Veterans Affairs, usually referred to as the VA.

ETS   Estimated Termination from Service; discharge day.

Fonda, Jane   Supporting the anti-war movement of the 1960s and 1970s, Fonda is vilified by many Vietnam veterans for visiting the North Vietnamese during the war and being photographed smiling in their company while sitting on an enemy anti-aircraft gun.

FNG   Vietnam war slang; Fucking New Guy.

freedom bird   Chartered passenger aircraft (usually Boeing 707) which ferried returning troops "to freedom" after finishing their tour of duty in Vietnam. Military aircraft were used to return wounded on litters.

"fuck-you" lizard   A Gecko lizard, which made a sound similar to "fuck-you" in English. Asians believed seven "fuck-yous" in a row was good luck.

gooks   Derogatory slang usually meaning an Asian enemy, but often used to refer to any Asian.

Green Machine   Slang referring to the United States Marine Corps.

grunt   USA and USMC slang for an infantryman, also ground-pounder.

Gung Ho   Chinese, "Work Together." The motto of the Marine Raiders during World War II, its meaning has been extended to convey fighting spirit as well as loyalty.

Ho Bo Woods   Densely forested area in III Corps, Vietnam, near the Cambodian Border. Held in strength by the VC and heavily contested by US and ARVN forces. Heavy fighting at the beginning of the war made it a graveyard of equipment.

Hueys   A single-engine, single-rotor light attack/observation helicopter noted for maneuverability and firepower. Larger models were used, primarily by the Army for gunship support, troop transport, and medical evacuation. Smaller models were used, primarily by Marines, for gunship support, observation, and emergency medevacs.

in country   Slang usually meaning being anywhere in the Republic of South Vietnam; and not simply "in the country," as opposed to "the city."

Inchon   South Korean seaport near Seoul, site of amphibious landing by General Douglas MacArthur in September 1950.

Indian country   Any area occupied by enemy forces.

IV   Intravenous feeding of plasma, blood, dextrose, or medicine through a tube-fed needle.

Iwo Jima   One of the Volcano Islands of Japan, Iwo Jima was assaulted by the 4th and 5th Marine Divisions on February 19, 1945 with the objective of capturing two operational Japanese airfields and one airfield under construction in order to deny these bases to the enemy to use them in their island-hopping campaign. Marine losses numbered 4,644 killed and 17,328 wounded in 35 days of unrelenting combat. Only 216 of the 20,000 Japanese defenders survived.

jungle rot   Fungal infections of the feet due to long immersion in swamp water.

kamikaze Japanese for "Divine Wind," suicide aircraft whose pilots crashed themselves into allied warships near the end of WW II. The heaviest attacks occurred during the battle for Okinawa.

Kent State University, Kent, Ohio On May 4, 1970, four students were killed by National Guardsmen as 3,000 anti-war protesters rallied on the commons in the center of the campus.

Khe Sanh Remote American airbase on the Laotian boarder near the Demilitarized Zone (DMZ) that separated North and South Vietnam. The base was beleaguered by strong NVA forces in January 1968. Cut off from resupply by land, the 26th Marine Regiment was supported and supplied by air throughout the battle.

KIA Killed in Action.

Klonopin An anticonvulsant medication used for treating people diagnosed with PTSD. It is helpful in some cases for reducing aggressive impulses.

Krauts Derogatory term referring to a German national, stems from "Sauerkraut."

Laos Borders North and South Vietnam on the west, used by the enemy to stage troops and run supplies during the Vietnam War.

LCVP Landing Craft, Vehicle, Personnel; a small craft with a bow ramp used to transport troops and light vehicles from ship to shore.

leech hole A place that sucked life and feeling from a person.

low crawling A low-profile method of traversing terrain that maintains the limbs and torso in contact with the ground in order to avoid enemy fire or detection. The arm and leg on each side of the body are moved in unison to propel oneself forward.

LP Listening Post, a one- or two-man outpost set beyond the perimeter of a base to give advance warning on enemy infiltrators.

LST Landing Ship Tank, designed to transport heavy vehicles and land them directly onto a beach.

LT Pronounced "Ell-Tee," slang for lieutenant.

Lupus A chronic skin disease. One form attacks other body systems, especially the circulatory system, and can be fatal.

LZ Landing zone for inserting troops by air in enemy territory.

M-14 Standard infantry weapon during the early years of Vietnam, firing a 7.62 mm NATO round from a 20-round magazine. Wt. 12 lbs.

M-16 Replaced the M-14 as the standard infantry weapon, firing a 5.56 mm NATO round from a 20 round magazine. Wt. 3.1 lbs. Early models jammed in action, motivating troops to "appropriate" the older model M-14 issued to main base troops.

M-60   Standard light machine gun of U.S. troops and helicopters in Vietnam, firing a 7.62 mm NATO round.

March Hares   From **Alice in Wonderland**, "mad as a March Hare."

MIA   Missing in Action.

Nachshon (Nachun)   The chief sorcerer and oracle of the Tibetan government; an incarnation of a god of the Turki tribes, made the religious guardian of the first monastery. Once a year, the nachun goes to Lhasa to prophesy the events of the coming year. He and other sorcerers accompany troops into battle to interpret portents.

Napoleon-Saline   An amphibious operation conducted by Marines of the 1st Amphibious Tractor Battalion near the Cua Viet River (just south of the Demilitarized Zone) in November and December 1967.

Navane   A drug used to control psychosis.

numbing   A conscious or unconscious effort to shut out painful memories, sometimes through the use of drugs or alcohol, but often through psychic numbing, where the vet believes he or she has lost the ability to feel. In combat, a veteran cannot take the time to allow a strong emotion to develop into "feeling." Vets often tell of incidents where they did not "feel anything" about the death of a friend, the loss of a patient, the killing of an enemy, or even the death of innocent civilians. In later years a fear of feeling may develop, and vets can find it uncomfortable to demonstrate love or compassion for family; they find "feeling anything" frightening, since feeling seems tied to recalling painful memories.

nuoc mam   Vietnamese fish sauce, buried and allowed to age.

NVA   North Vietnamese Army, equally used in referring to a North Vietnamese soldier.

Okinawa   The largest island in the Ryukyus, Okinawa was assaulted by a combined Army-Marine force on April 1, 1945. Okinawa, lying 350 nautical miles from Kyushu, Japan, 330 miles from Formosa and 450 miles from Shanghai, was a strategic base from which assault troops could prepare for the invasion of Japan. Though the landing was unopposed, Okinawa is an island of rugged hills pocked with caves, and American infantry units fought a grueling, 80-day battle into late June 1945, when the Japanese commanders Ushijima and Cho committed hara-kiri. Offshore, 1,900 suicide missions were flown against U.S. Navy ships.

OPM   Office of Personnel Management.

Parris Island   The U.S. Marine Corps Recruit Depot in South Carolina, provides "boot training" to most enlistees east of the Mississippi.

Phu Bai   A main American airbase in Thua Thien Province, South Vietnam (Northern I Corps).

Piva Forks, Torokina   The northern attack force of the 1st Marine Amphibious Force, consisting of the 3rd Marine Division, 1st Parachute Regiment, 2nd Raider Regiment and 3rd Defense Battalion assaulted Bougainville, the largest of the Solomon Islands, at Cape Torokina on November 1, 1943. The objective was to neutralize new enemy airfields and move closer to the main Japanese supply base at Rabaul. Marines fought fierce battles in the coconut groves of the Mission-Piva Trail, the Torokina River, on Hand Grenade Hill, and Hellzapoppin' Ridge.

point-man   The first man in a patrol, often scouting alone a short distance ahead of the rest of his unit to warn it of enemy presence. The point-man had to be on lookout for ambushes and booby traps, and could easily be cut off from his unit when the enemy opened fire.

police-up   Clean up trash, or remove useful material from a base or encampment.

POW   Prisoner of War.

PTSD   Post-Traumatic Stress Disorder.

Purple Heart   The first U.S. military decoration, instituted by George Washington in 1782 and awarded for bravery in action. Records indicate that only three men received it during the Revolutionary War, all noncommissioned officers. The original medal, sewn onto the coat, was a simple purple heart-shaped piece of cloth edged with silver braid. The award then fell into disuse for 150 years, and was revived on Washington's 200th birthday in 1932. The Purple Heart is now awarded to those wounded or killed (awarded posthumously) in the service of their country. The front of the medal depicts Washington in the uniform of a Continental Army general. The reverse has the inscription "For Military Merit" and the recipient's name.

RLT   Regimental Landing Team.

rock apes   Apes said to inhabit the rocky precipices often used by American soldiers as observation posts.

rotors   Helicopter blades. First used for observation and medical evacuation in Korea, and for close-air gunship support as well in Vietnam. The characteristic "whop-whop-whop" of the blades striking the air often evokes medical emergency or combat action and can be a trigger to flashbacks.

Saigon tea   Colored water or tea served to Saigon "bar girls," but charged to Americans at alcohol prices in return for the girls' "conversation."

salt   Navy term, "old salt": someone who had been around.

SAM   Surface-to-Air Missiles.

Semper Fi   Contraction of the USMC motto **Semper Fidelis** (Always Faithful) and a common greeting among former Marines.

SLF Special Landing Force.

Special Operations Clandestine operations, or any operations outside the scope of "normal" combat operations, often carried out behind enemy lines or within the civilian population.

Suribachi Cave-riddled inactive volcano commanding Iwo Jima Island. The flag raised by 5th Marine Division on Mount Suribachi was captured by photographer Joseph Rosenthal and memorialized in the Felix De Weldon monument near Arlington National Cemetery in Arlington, Virginia.

survival guilt Guilt over surviving the loss of comrades, or failing to save a life during combat. Vets sometimes withdraw or grow angry when told by a civilian how "lucky they are" to have survived the war. Rather than feeling "lucky," the vet often agonizes over why he or she was allowed to live; survival equates to personal and unforgivable failure.

Tan Son Nhut Main U.S. airbase near Saigon.

Tet Vietnamese lunar new year, the most important Vietnamese national holiday. At dawn on January 30, 1968, the first day of the Tet truce, Vietcong and NVA forces launched the largest offensive of the war against South Vietnam's seven largest cities. By February 10, the offensive was crushed in heavy fighting. Although a U.S. victory, the media focus on U.S. casualties was a psychological and political disaster for the U.S. conduct of the war. On February 22, 1969, after yet another Tet cease-fire ended, Communist forces began a second general offensive, attacking Saigon and 70 other cities and military positions.

Trilafon A drug used to control psychosis.

VC Viet Cong, refers to Communist guerrillas in South Vietnam; a contraction of the Vietnamese phrase meaning "Vietnamese Communists."

vet center The Department of Veterans Affairs' Readjustment Counseling Service operates nearly 200 Veteran Outreach Centers throughout the United States. These community-based centers are staffed by trained counselors and psychologists, many of them combat veterans, who provide one-on-one counseling and group therapy sessions to combat veterans who suffer from PTSD, or are otherwise in need of assistance. Their motto is "Help without Hassles."

Wall Vietnam Veterans Memorial in Washington, D.C., a black granite wall inscribed with the names of those killed and missing in the Vietnam War. Since its dedication in 1982, the Wall has been visited by countless veterans and their families as part of their healing process.

Women's Memorial Vietnam Women's Memorial depicting nurses caring for a wounded man, dedicated in 1992.

Xanax A drug used to control anxiety.

CONTRIBUTORS

About the Sidran Foundation

The Sidran Foundation is a publicly-supported, non-profit organization devoted to advocacy, education and research in support of people with psychiatric disabilities. The foundation is particularly interested in providing support and advocating empowerment for people who have survived psychological trauma, and has developed resources in this area. The Sidran Foundation Bookshelf is a mail-order book service providing annotated catalogs and home-delivery of books, audio and video tapes, and informational materials of particular interest to trauma survivors, their supportive family and friends, and their therapists. The Sidran Press is publisher of a number of books and informational brochures on psychological trauma topics, including the highly acclaimed *Multiple Personality Disorder From the Inside Out,* a collection of writings about living with MPD by 146 survivors and their significant others. In addition, Sidran has compiled an extensive database of trauma support and treatment resources and conducts educational workshops. For more information, contact The Sidran Foundation and Press, 2328 W. Joppa Road, Suite 15, Lutherville, MD, 21093; phone: (410) 825-8888 and fax: (410) 337-0747.